The New Illustrated

SONGBOOK

Foreword by Steven Spielberg

Hal Leonard Publishing Corporation,
Milwaukee, Wisconsin

The New Illustrated

Disney

SONGBOOK

Harry N. Abrams, Inc.,
Publishers, New York

Endpapers: Two representative examples of "bar sheets,"
which govern the entire sound track of a movie.

Project Manager: Lois Brown
Designer: Darilyn Lowe

For Hal Leonard Publishing Corporation: Glenda Herro, Managing Editor, Book Division

Music engraving by Hal Leonard Publishing Corporation, Milwaukee, Wisconsin

Library of Congress Cataloging-in-Publication Data
The new illustrated Disney songbook.

  1. vocal score.
  For voice and piano.
  Summary: Presents in sheet music format about
eighty songs from such Walt Disney movies as
"Cinderella," "Dumbo," and "Mary Poppins."
  1. Children's songs. 2. Moving-picture music—
Excerpts—Vocal scores with piano. [1. Songs. 2. Motion
picture music] I. Disney, Walt, 1901–1966. II. Walt
Disney Productions.
M1997.N437 1986   86-750676
ISBN 0-8109-0846-8 (Abrams)
ISBN 0-88188-467-7 (Hal Leonard)

Times Mirror Books

Printed and bound in Italy

Contents

Foreword

Walt Disney, whom I like to think of as the surrogate father of the "baby boomer" generation, was a man of indisputable wisdom and vision. He also possessed a remarkable ear for selecting music—both as to how it would work in his films and as to the types of songs that would invariably appeal to the American public at large.

I can't think of a single animated Disney feature that doesn't immediately associate itself with a song, nor can I think of a Disney song that doesn't inspire instant recognition of the Disney film from which it originated.

Beyond the technical problems of integrating music and film that Walt and his staff wrestled with and solved, I believe his greatest achievement was elevating music beyond its earlier role of mere accompaniment to the screen action. The perfection of the synchronization of music and movement, particularly in the cartoons of the thirties, serves as a symbol of the era of American craftsmanship.

Above all, Walt emphasized a sort of wistful optimism in his films, which I believe contributed to the American audience's perception of Disney films as the place where dreams and their fulfillment were within the reach of all dreamers. The word "dream" in relation to Walt Disney has probably been overused, but I think it illustrates that Walt was vitally aware that by appealing to people's strong desire to wish and dream, he would always have a central connection where it counted most... in their hearts.

The "baby boomers" did not necessarily grow up whistling the magnificent themes of Rodgers and Hammerstein, or Ira and George Gershwin. We had the music and lyrics memorized from "Give a Little Whistle," "Zip-A-Dee-Doo-Dah," "Bibbidi-Bobbidi-Boo," "When You Wish upon a Star," "Supercalifragilisticexpialidocious," and even though Ned Washington, Leigh Harline, Ray Gilbert, Allie Wrubel, Mack David, Al Hoffman, Jerry Livingston, Richard Sherman, and Robert Sherman were not generally thought of as household names, their music touched our hearts and gave us the songs of our earliest memories that we and our children must never forget.

Steven Spielberg
March 6, 1986

The New Illustrated

Disney
SONGBOOK

ain't a bet-ter thing than a tune, Than a tune, You can whis - tle

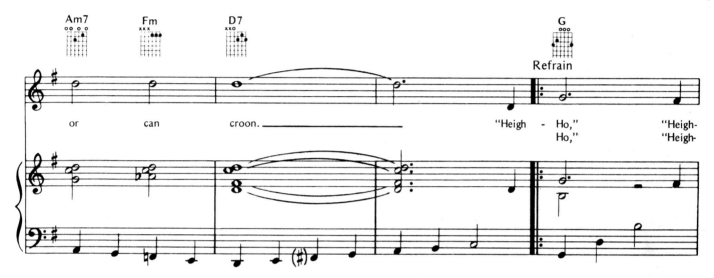

or can croon. _____ "Heigh - Ho," "Heigh-
Ho," "Heigh-

Refrain

Heigh-Ho

From Walt Disney's
Snow White and the Seven Dwarfs

Words by Larry Morey
Music by Frank Churchill

I'm Wishing

From Walt Disney's
Snow White and the Seven Dwarfs

Words by Larry Morey
Music by Frank Churchill

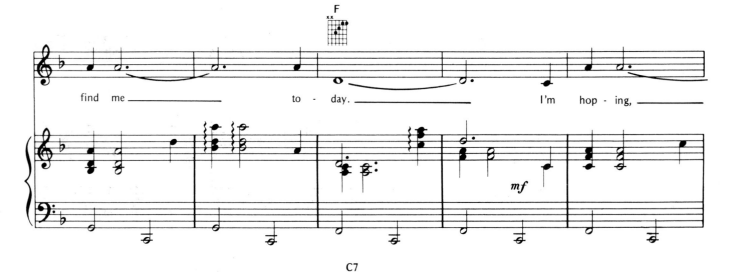

Lyrics:

I'm wish-ing _____ for the one I love to find me _____ to-day. _____ I'm hop-ing, _____ And I'm dream-ing of the nice things, _____ he'll

say. _____ Tell me, Wish-ing Well, _____ Will my wish come true? _____

With your mag - ic spell, _____ Won't you tell my loved one what to

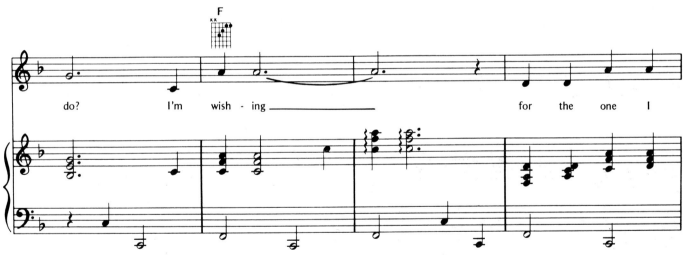

do? I'm wish - ing _____ for the one I

love to find me _____ to - day. _____

17

One Song

From Walt Disney's
Snow White and the Seven Dwarfs

Words by Larry Morey
Music by Frank Churchill

With a song I come to you, Like a trou-ba-dour, With a sim-ple ser-e-nade,

That, and noth-ing more. I have no lute to play. No tink-ling gui-tar.

Just a song to tell you, How sweet to me you are. One song, I have but

Some Day My Prince Will Come

From Walt Disney's
Snow White and the Seven Dwarfs

Words by Larry Morey
Music by Frank Churchill

He'll whis-per "I love you,"
Some day we'll say and do,

And steal a kiss or two, Though he's far a-
Things we've been long-ing to, Though she's far a-

way, I'll find my love some day, Some day when my dreams come
way, I'll find my love some day, Some day when my dreams come

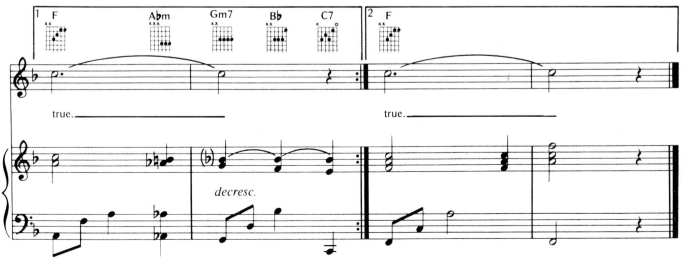

true._____

true._____

21

Whistle While You Work

From Walt Disney's
Snow White and the Seven Dwarfs

Words by Larry Morey
Music by Frank Churchill

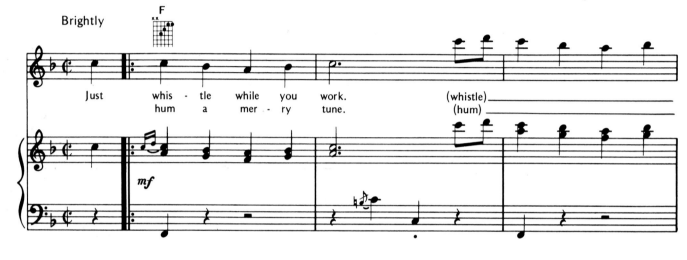

Just whis-tle while you work. (whistle)
hum a mer-ry tune. (hum)

Put on that grin and start right in, To whis-tle loud and
Just do your best and then take a rest, And sing your-self a

long. Just song. When there's too much to do, Don't

let it both-er you, For-get your trou-bles, Try to be just

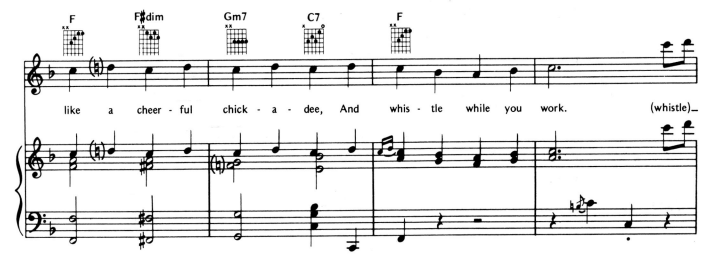

like a cheer-ful chick-a-dee, And whis-tle while you work. (whistle)___

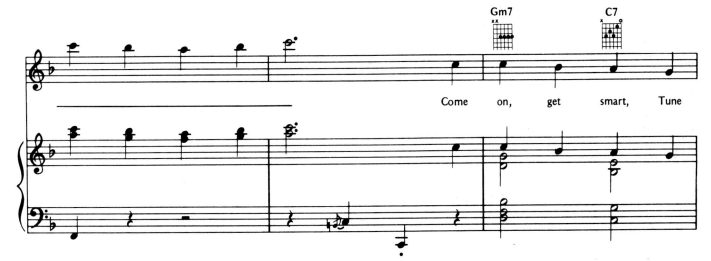

Come on, get smart, Tune

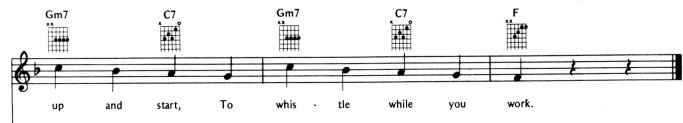

up and start, To whis-tle while you work.

With a Smile and a Song

From Walt Disney's *Snow White and the Seven Dwarfs*

Words by Larry Morey
Music by Frank Churchill

With a smile and a song, Life is just like a
With a smile and a song, All the world seems to

bright sun-ny day, Your cares fade a - way,_____ And your heart is
wak - en a - new, Re - joic - ing with you,_____ As the song is

young.

sung.

25

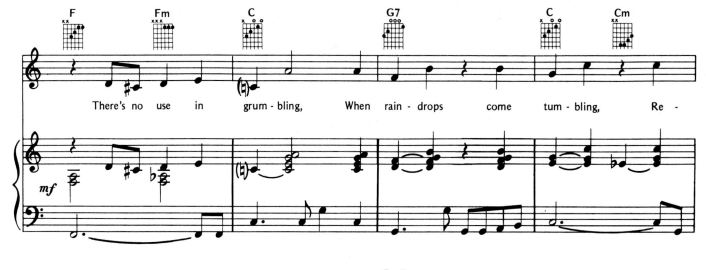

There's no use in grum-bling, When rain-drops come tum-bling, Re-

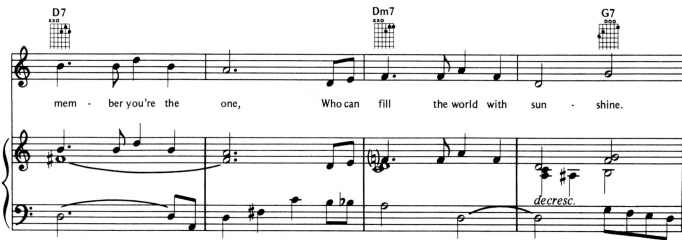

mem - ber you're the one, Who can fill the world with sun - shine.

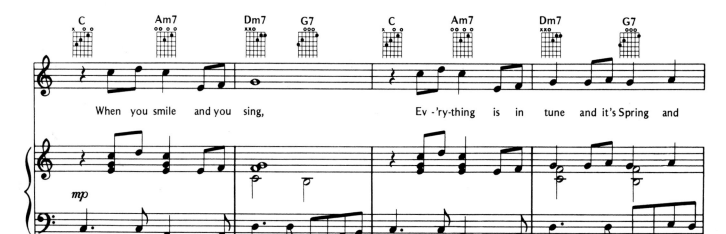

When you smile and you sing, Ev-'ry-thing is in tune and it's Spring and

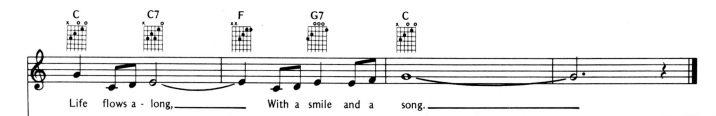

Life flows a - long,_____ With a smile and a song._____

Minnie's Yoo Hoo

Words by Walt Disney and Carl Stalling
Music by Carl Stalling

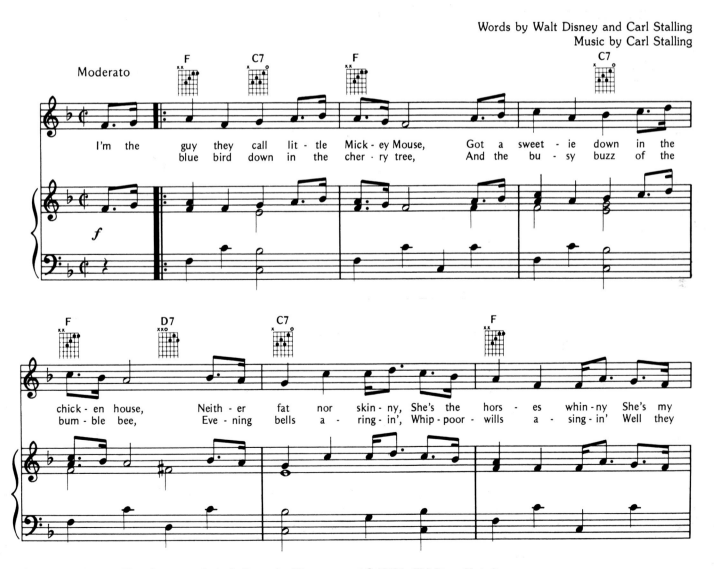

I'm the guy they call lit-tle Mick-ey Mouse, Got a sweet-ie down in the
blue bird down in the cher-ry tree, And the bu-sy buzz of the

chick-en house, Neith-er fat nor skin-ny, She's the hors-es whin-ny She's my
bum-ble bee, Eve-ning bells a - ring-in', Whip-poor-wills a - sing-in' Well they

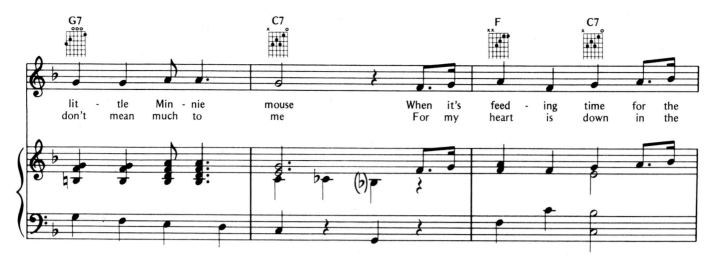

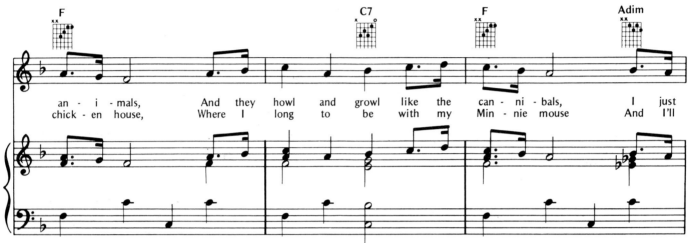

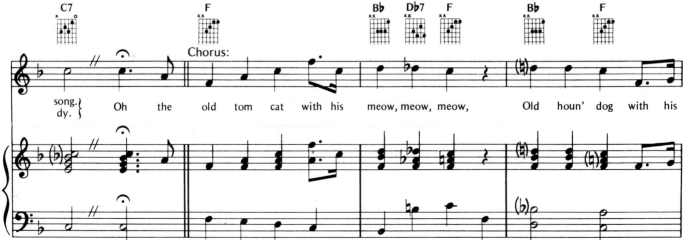

bow, wow, wow, The crows caw, caw, and the mule's hee - haw Gosh what a rack-et like an

old buzz saw, I have list-ened to the Koo-koo kook his koo - koo, And I've

heard the roos-ter cock his doo-dle doo doo, With the cows and the chick-ens, they all

sound like the dick-ens, When I hear my lit-tle Min-nie's yoo hoo. Oh the yoo hoo.

The World Owes Me a Living

From Walt Disney's Silly Symphony,
The Grasshopper and the Ants

Words by Larry Morey
Music by Leigh Harline

There once was an old grass-hop-per who could on-ly think of fun, He

looked on work as some-thing too un-pleas-ant to be done. He loved to sit in the

sum-mer sun and fid-dle all day long. While doz-ing there he'd play this air, And

sing this lit - tle song. "Oh the world owes me a liv - ing,
Dee - dle, die - dle, doe - dle - die - dle

dum, Oh, the world owes me a liv - ing,
Dee - dle, die - dle, doe - dle - die - dle

dum. If I worked hard all day. I must sleep bet - ter when in

bed at night, I sleep all day so that's all right,
Dee - dle, die - dle, doe - dle - die - dle dum.

31

Who's Afraid of the Big Bad Wolf?

From Walt Disney's *Three Little Pigs*

Words and Music by Frank Churchill
Additional lyric by Ann Ronell

ver-y bad _ wolf, they _ did-n't give three figs, Num - ber one was ver - y gay, and he

built his house with hay; With a hey hey toot, he blew on his flute and he played a - round all

day. Who's a - fraid of the big bad wolf, big bad wolf,

big bad wolf? Who's a - fraid of the big bad wolf? Tra - la - la - la - la.

Give a Little Whistle

From Walt Disney's *Pinocchio*

Words by Ned Washington
Music by Leigh Harline

When you get in trou-ble and you don't know right from wrong;
When you meet temp-ta-tion, and the urge is ver-y strong;
Give a lit-tle

whis-tle! (Whistle ____) Give a lit-tle whis-tle! (Whistle ____)

____) Not just a lit-tle squeak; Puck-er up and

Hi-Diddle-Dee-Dee
(An Actor's Life For Me)

From Walt Disney's *Pinocchio*

Words by Ned Washington
Music by Leigh Harline

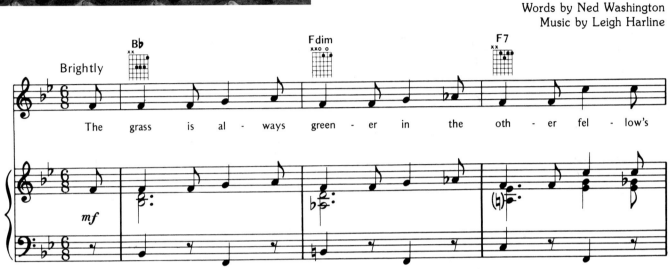

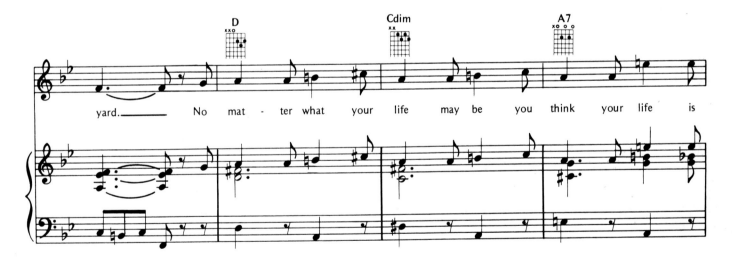

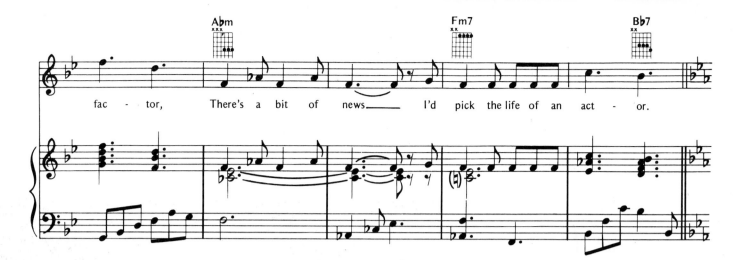

fac - tor, There's a bit of news____ I'd pick the life of an act - or.

Hi - did - dle - dee - dee____ An act - or's life for me____ A high silk hat and a
Hi - did - dle - dee - dee____ You sleep till af - ter two,____ You prom - e - nade with a

sil - ver cane, A watch of gold with a dia - mond chain.
big cig - ar, You tour the world in a pri - vate car, You

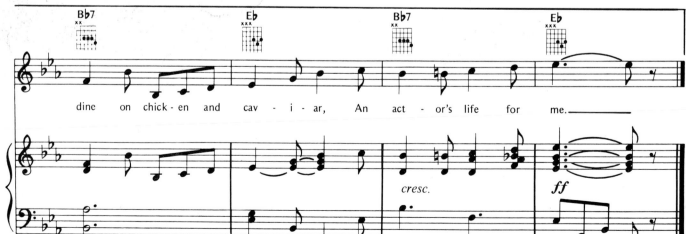

dine on chick - en and cav - i - ar, An act - or's life for me.____

I've Got No Strings

From Walt Disney's *Pinocchio*

Words by Ned Washington
Music by Leigh Harline

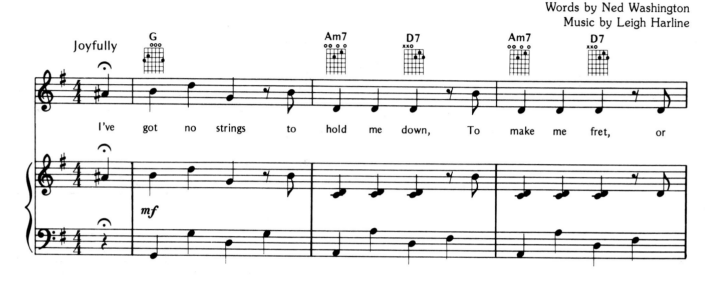

I've got no strings to hold me down, To make me fret, or

make me frown, I had strings But now I'm free, There

are no strings on me. Hi o the

me - ri - o, I'm as hap - py as can be.

I want the world to know Noth-ing ev - er wor - ries me. I've

got no strings so I have fun, I'm not tied up to an - y - one,

How I love my li - ber - ty, There are no strings on me.

41

When You Wish upon a Star

From Walt Disney's *Pinocchio*

Words by Ned Washington
Music by Leigh Harline

Slowly, with expression

When you wish up - on a star, makes no diff - 'rence
If your heart is in your dream, no re - quest is

who you are, An - y - thing your heart de - sires will
too ex - treme, When you wish up - on a star as

come to you.
dream - ers
do. Fate is

43

Baby Mine

From Walt Disney's *Dumbo*

Words by Ned Washington
Music by Frank Churchill

Moderately Slow

Ba - by mine _____ don't you cry _____
Lit - tle one _____ when you play _____

Ba - by mine _____ dry your eye _____
Don't you mind _____ what you say _____

Rest your head close to my heart, Nev - er to part, Ba - by of
Let those eyes spar - kle and shine, Nev - er a tear, Ba - by of

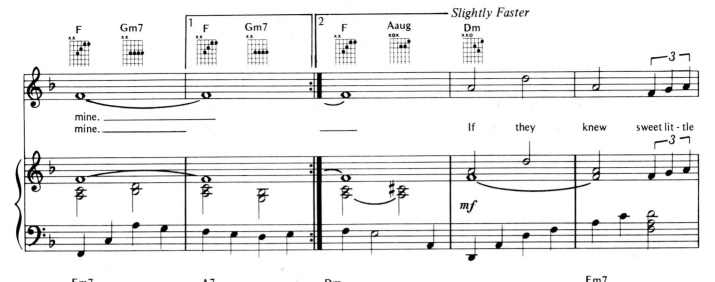

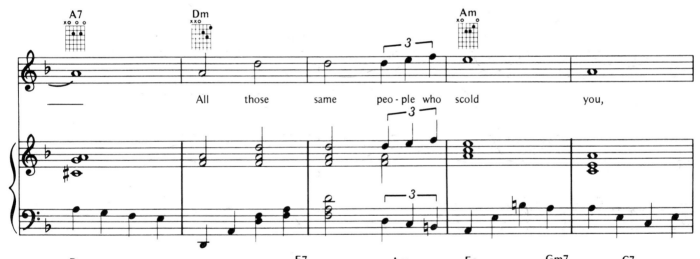

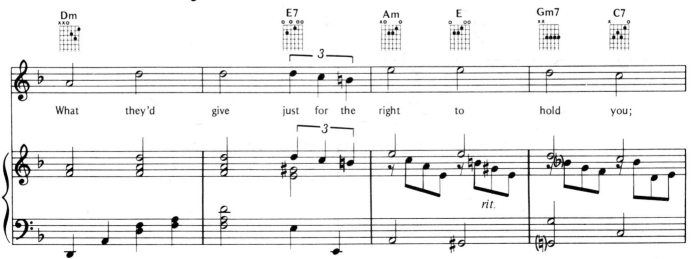

45

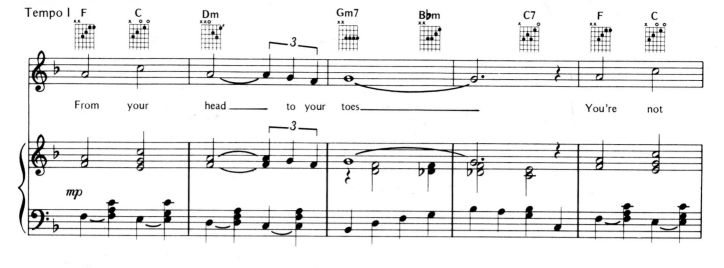

From your head ___ to your toes ___ You're not

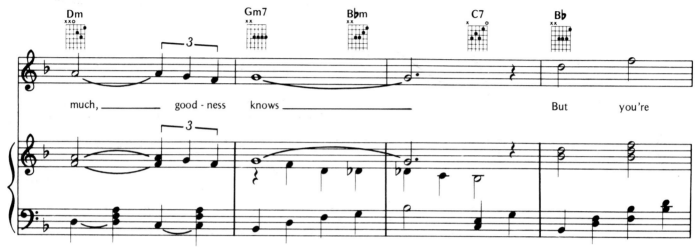

much, ___ good-ness knows ___ But you're

so pre-cious to me, Cute as can be, Ba-by of mine. ___

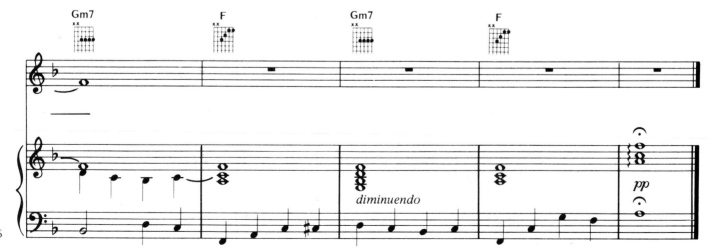

Casey Junior

From Walt Disney's *Dumbo*

Words by Ned Washington
Music by Frank Churchill

It's Cas - ey Jun - ior, com - in' down' the track__
Hear him puff - in' _____ 'round the hill__

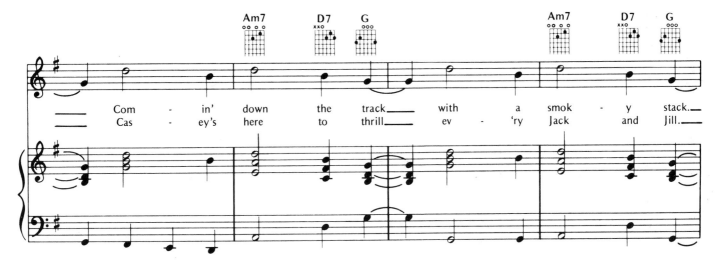

Com - in' down the track____ with a smok - y stack.__
Cas - ey's here to thrill____ ev - 'ry Jack and Jill.__

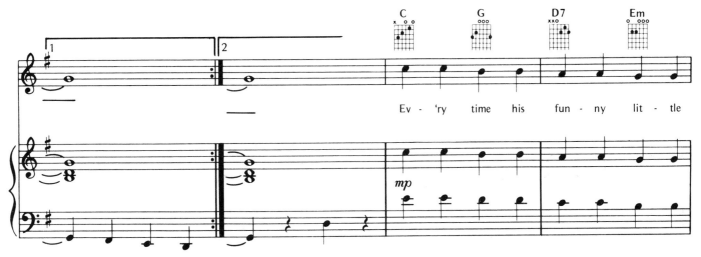

Ev - 'ry time his fun - ny lit - tle

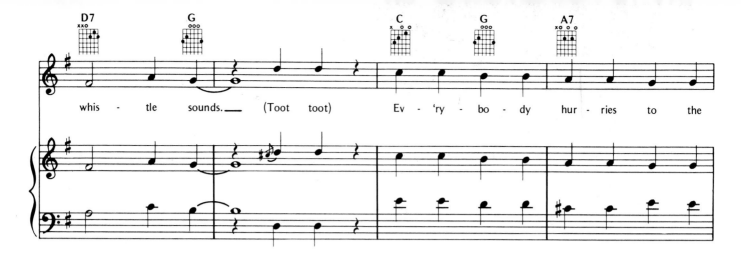

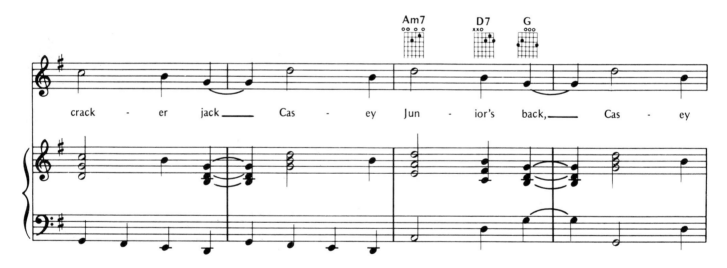

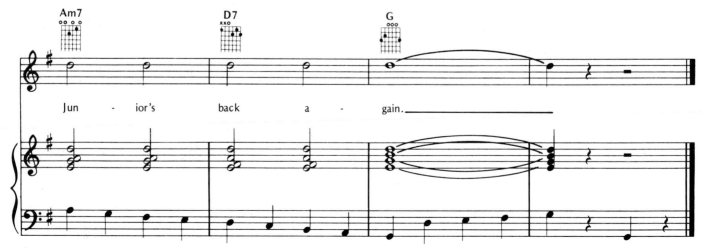

48

Pink Elephants on Parade

From Walt Disney's *Dumbo*

Words by Ned Washington
Music by Oliver Wallace

Briskly

1. Look out! Look out! Pink el - e - phants on pa - rade,
2. Look out! Look out! They're walk - ing a - round the bed,

Here they come! Hip - pe - ty hop - pe - ty, they're here and there, Pink
on their head, Clip - pe - ty clop - pe - ty, ar - rayed in braid, Pink

49

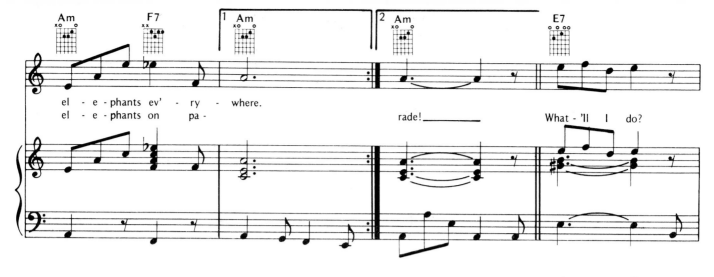

el - e -phants ev' -ry - where.
el - e -phants on pa - rade!_____ What - 'll I do?

What - 'll I do? What an un - u - su - al view!

1. I can stand the
2. I am not the

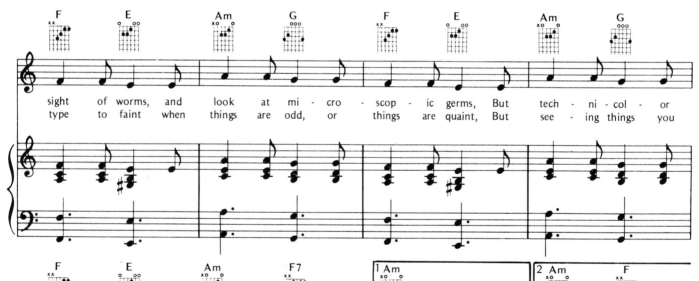

sight of worms, and look at mi - cro - scop - ic germs, But tech - ni - col - or
type to faint when things are odd, or things are quaint, But see - ing things you

pach - y - derms is real - ly too much___ for me.___
know that ain't can cer - tain -ly give you an aw - ful fright!

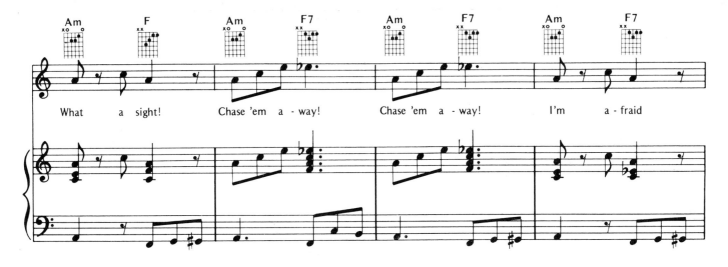

What a sight! Chase 'em a-way! Chase 'em a-way! I'm a-fraid

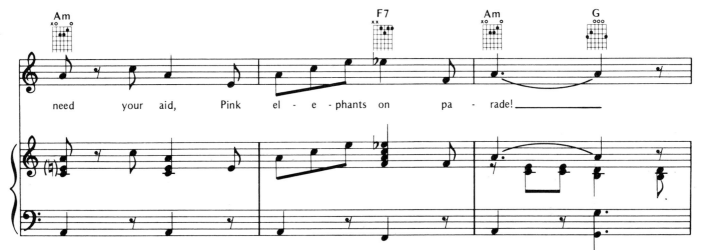

need your aid, Pink el-e-phants on pa-rade! _____

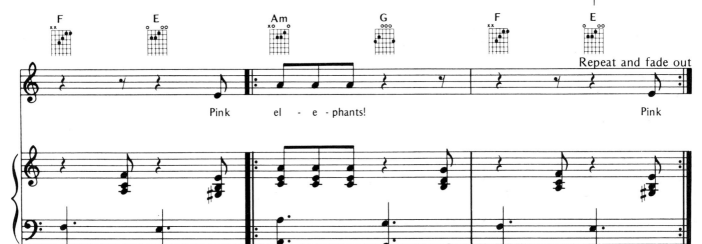

Repeat and fade out

Pink el-e-phants! Pink

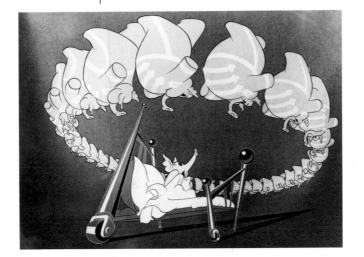

51

When I See an Elephant Fly

From Walt Disney's *Dumbo*

Words by Ned Washington
Music by Oliver Wallace

went in-to a store, saw a bi-cy-cle shop.__ You can't de-ny__ the
things that you see,__ But I know there's cer - tain things that just can't be.__ The oth - er
day by chance,__ saw an old barn dance,__ And I just laugh'd till I thought__ I'd die But I
think I will have seen ev-'ry-thing__ When I see an el - e-phant fly.__

Little
April Shower

From Walt Disney's *Bambi*

Words by Larry Morey
Music by Frank Churchill

Moderato

Drip, drip, drop, lit-tle A-pril show-er, beat-ing a tune as you
Drip, drip, drop, lit-tle A-pril show-er, beat-ing a tune ev-'ry-

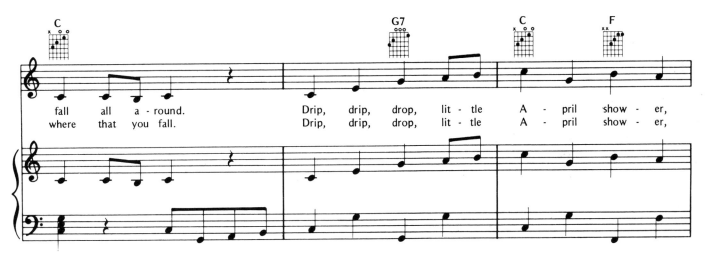

fall all a-round. Drip, drip, drop, lit-tle A-pril show-er,
where that you fall. Drip, drip, drop, lit-tle A-pril show-er,

what can com-pare with your beau-ti-ful sound. Drip, drip, drop, when the
I'm get-ting wet and I don't care at all.

To Coda

sky is cloud - y your pret - ty mu - sic can bright - en the day.

D.C. al Coda

Drip, drip, drop, when the sun says, "How - dy" you say "Good-bye" right a - way._____

CODA

Drip! Drop! Drip! Drop! I'll nev - er be a - fraid of a

good lit - tle gay lit - tle A - pril ser - e - nade._____

Love Is a Song

From Walt Disney's *Bambi*

Words by Larry Morey
Music by Frank Churchill

Love is a song that never er
Love is a song that never er

ends.
ends.

Life may be swift and
One sim - ple theme and re -

Zip-A-Dee-Doo-Dah

From Walt Disney's *Song of the South*

Words by Ray Gilbert
Music by Allie Wrubel

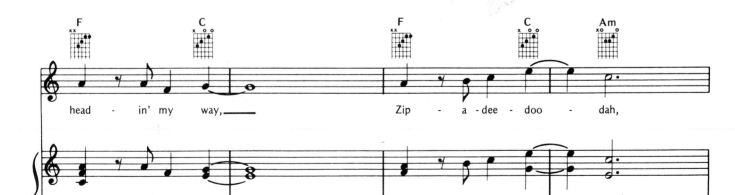

Lyrics:
Zip - a-dee-doo - dah, Zip - a-dee - ay,____ My, oh my,____ what a won-der-ful day!____ Plen - ty of sun - shine, head - in' my way,____ Zip - a-dee-doo - dah,

Zip - a - dee - ay! ___ Mis - ter Blue - bird on my shoul - der, ___

___ It's the truth, it's "act - ch'll", Ev - 'ry - thing is

mp   *cresc.*   *decresc.*   TACET

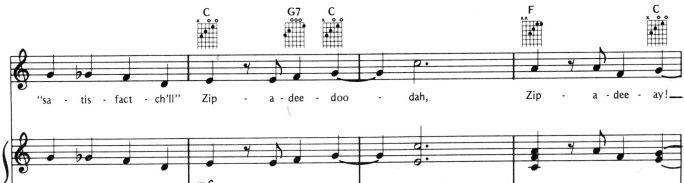

"sa - tis - fact - ch'll" Zip - a - dee - doo - dah, Zip - a - dee - ay! ___

mf

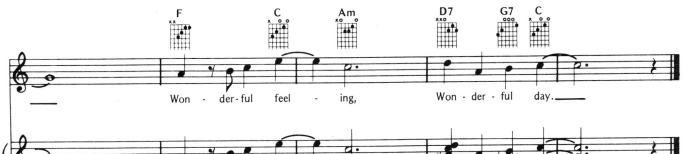

___ Won - der - ful feel - ing, Won - der - ful day. ___

Lavender Blue
(Dilly Dilly)

From Walt Disney's *So Dear to My Heart*

Words by Larry Morey
Music by Eliot Daniel

Great grand - fa -ther met great grand-moth-er when she was a shy young miss, And great grand - fa -ther won great grand-moth-er with words more or less like this.

Lav - en - der blue dil -ly, dil -ly lav - en - der green;

pre - ty lit - tle church on a dil - ly, dil - ly day {You'll / I'll} be wed in a dil - ly, dil - ly dress of

lav - en - der blue dil - ly, dil - ly, lav - en - der green.

Then {I'll / you'll} be king, dil - ly, dil - ly, and {you'll / I'll} be {my / your}

queen. _____ queen. _____

Blue Shadows
on the Trail

From Walt Disney's *Melody Time*

Words by Johnny Lange
Music by Eliot Daniel

Blue shad-ows on the trail, _____

Blue moon shin-ing through the trees, _____ And a plain-tive

wail from the dis-tance _____ comes a-drift-in' on the

The Lord Is Good to Me

From Walt Disney's *Melody Time*

Words and Music by Kim Gannon
and Walter Kent

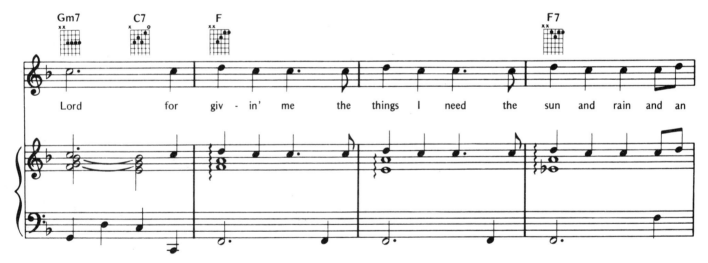

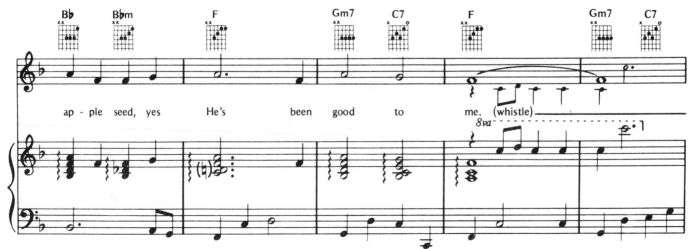

68

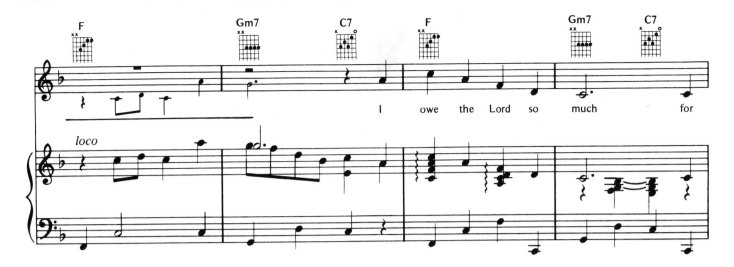

I owe the Lord so much for

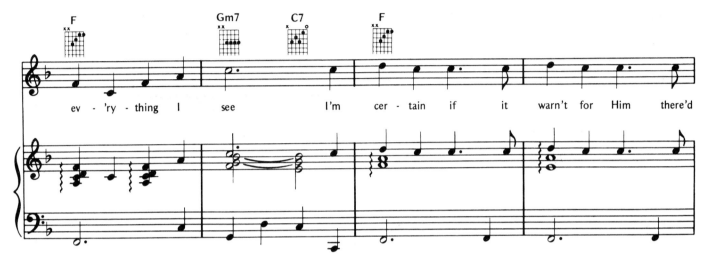

ev - 'ry - thing I see I'm cer - tain if it warn't for Him there'd

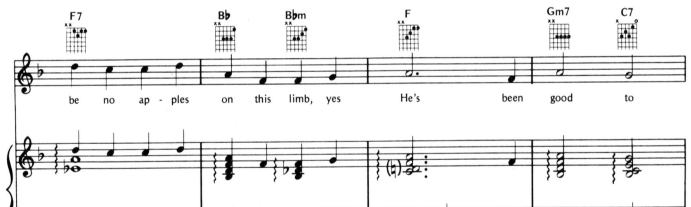

be no ap - ples on this limb, yes He's been good to

me. (whistle) _____ Oh here am I 'neath a blue, blue sky a-

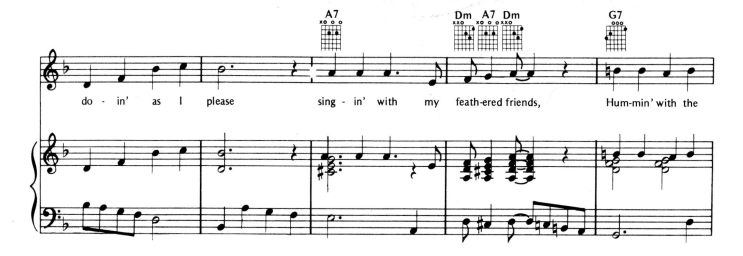

do - in' as I please   sing - in' with my feath-ered friends,   Hum-min' with the

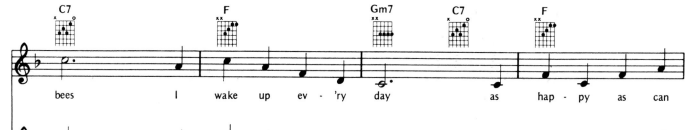

bees   I wake up ev -'ry day   as hap - py as can

be   be - cause I know that with His care my ap - ple trees they will

still be there, Oh the Lord's been good to me. (whistle)

A Dream Is a Wish Your Heart Makes

From Walt Disney's *Cinderella*

Words and Music by
Mack David, Al Hoffman and Jerry Livingston

Lyrics: A dream is a wish your heart makes____ When you're fast a - sleep.____ In dreams you will lose your heart - aches;____ What - ev - er you wish for, you

keep. Have faith in your dreams and some day ___

___ Your rain-bow will come smil - ing thru, ___

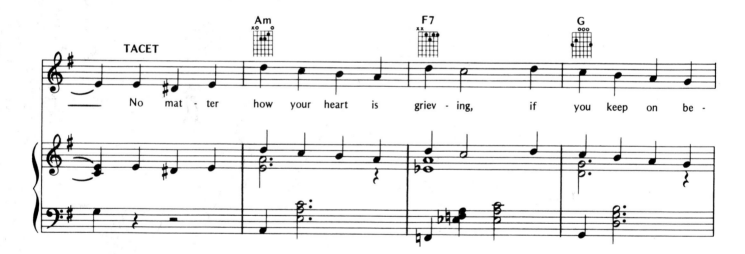

TACET

___ No mat - ter how your heart is griev - ing, if you keep on be -

liev - ing, the dream that you wish will come true. ___

dim.   mp

72

Bibbidi-Bobbidi-Boo
(The Magic Song)

From Walt Disney's *Cinderella*

Words by Jerry Livingston
Music by Mack David and Al Hoffman

bib - bi - di - bob - bi - di - boo. Sa - la - ga - doo - la means men - chic -ka boo - le - roo, But the

thing - a - ma -bob that does the job is bib - bi - di - bob - bi - di - boo. Sa - la - ga - doo - la men - chic -ka boo la

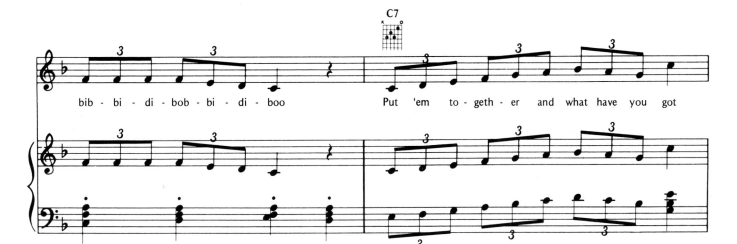

bib - bi - di - bob - bi - di - boo Put 'em to - geth - er and what have you got

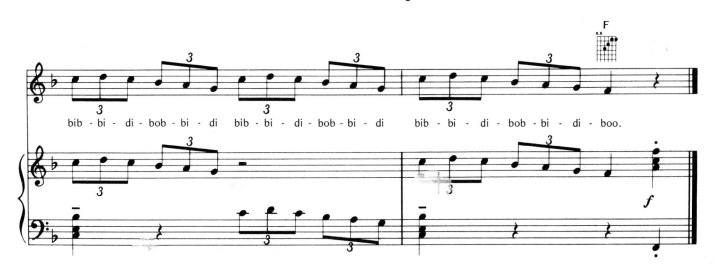

bib - bi - di - bob - bi - di bib - bi - di - bob - bi - di bib - bi - di - bob - bi - di - boo.

So This Is Love
(The Cinderella Waltz)

From Walt Disney's *Cinderella*

Words and Music by
Mack David, Al Hoffman and Jerry Livingston

So this is love, Mm ___ So this is love ___ So this is what makes life di - vine. ___ I'm all a - glow, Mm ___ And now I know ___ The key to all heav - en is

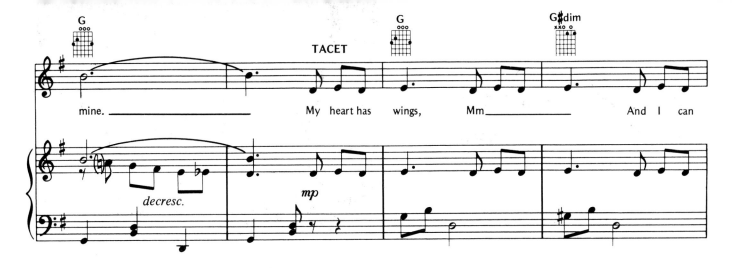

mine. _____ My heart has wings, Mm _____ And I can

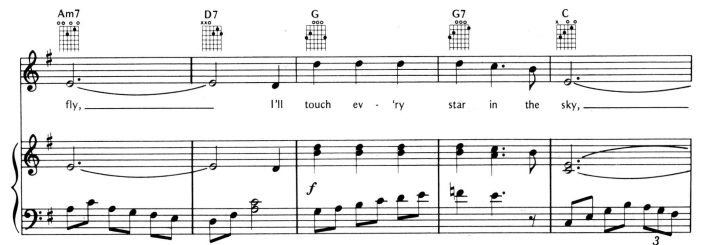

fly, _____ I'll touch ev - 'ry star in the sky, _____

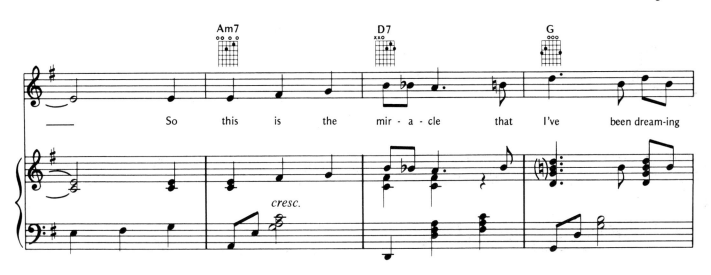

_____ So this is the mir - a - cle that I've been dream-ing

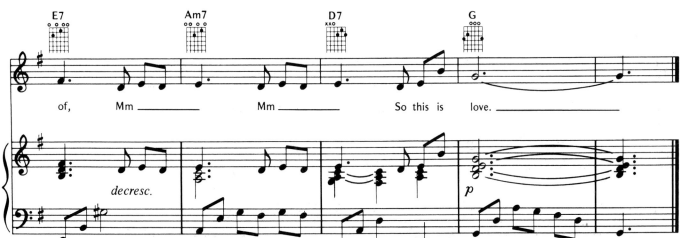

of, Mm _____ Mm _____ So this is love. _____

The Work Song

From Walt Disney's *Cinderella*

Words and Music by
Mack David, Al Hoffman and Jerry Livingston

Lyrics:

Cin- der- el- la, Cin- der- el- la, All I hear is Cin- der- el- la, from the mo- ment that I get up, till shades of night are fall- ing, There is- n't an- y let- up, I hear them call- ing,

call - ing "Go up and do the at - tic and go down and do the

cel - lar, you can do them both to - geth - er, Cin - der - el - la."

To Coda ⊕

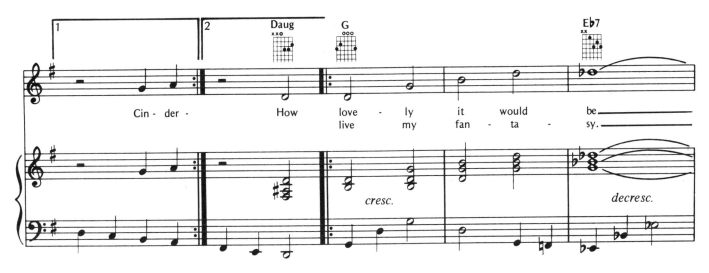

Cin - der -

How love - ly it would be_____

live my fan - ta - sy._____

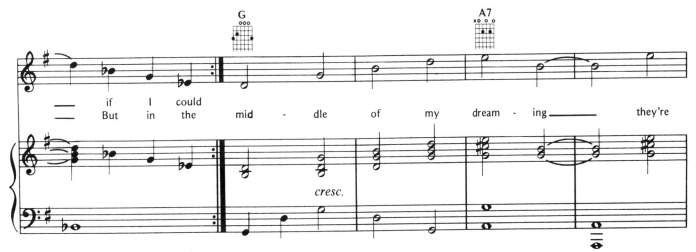

_____ if I could

_____ But in the mid - dle of my dream - ing_____ they're

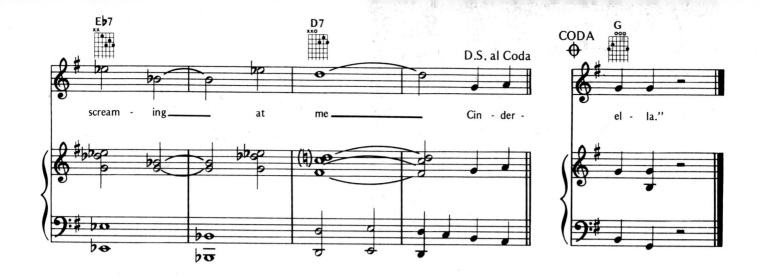

scream - ing ____ at me ____ Cin - der -

D.S. al Coda

CODA

el - la."

How D'ye Do and Shake Hands

From Walt Disney's *Alice in Wonderland*

Words by Cy Coben
Music by Oliver Wallace

1. You go through life and nev-er know the day when fate may
in-tro-duce your girl friend to your ver-y spe-cial

bring a sit-u-a-tion that will prove to
beau and then he does-n't call you and the

be em-bar-rass-ing, Your face gets red, you
next thing that you know You see them both a-

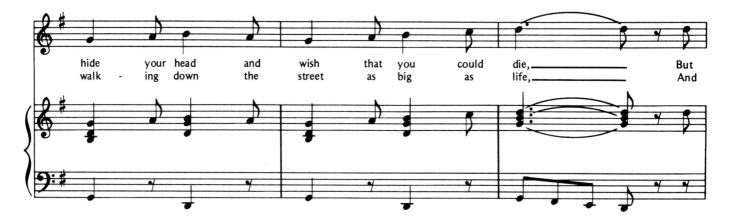

hide   your   head   and   wish   that   you   could   die,_____ But
walk - ing   down   and   the   wish   street   that   as   big   could   as   life,_____ And

that's   old   fash - ioned,   here's   a   new   thing   you   should   real - ly
when   he   says,   "My   dear,   I'd   like   to   have   you   meet   my

try, }   Say: "How d' ye do"   and   shake   hands,   shake   hands,
wife, }

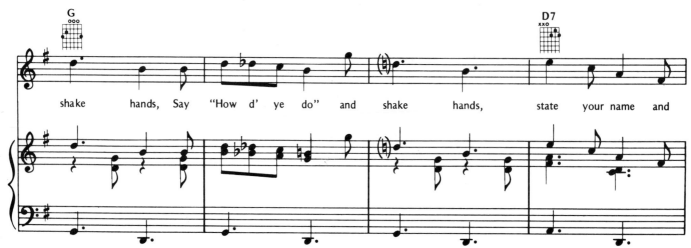

shake   hands,   Say "How d' ye do"   and   shake   hands,   state   your   name   and

3. You take your girl friend on a date and you have so much fun
   That you forget to bring her home until it's after one,
   Her father's waiting at the door as angry as can be,
   I've had that happen lots of times, so take this tip from me, say: *(Refrain)*

4. While at the wedding of some folks you hardly know by sight,
   And in a conversation with a woman on your right
   You say you think the bride's a mess, her face she ought to hide,
   And when you find you're talking to the mother of the bride, say:
   (Refrain)

5. While walking thru a cemetery very late at night
   You find that you're confronted by a figure dressed in white,
   And tho the blood inside your veins has quickly turned to ice
   Everything will be O.K. if you take my advice, say: *(Refrain)*

6. You walk into a restaurant as hungry as can be,
   And when you've had a meal of ev'rything from A to Z
   You realize you haven't got a single cent with you
   And when the manager comes over this is what you do, say: *(Refrain)*

7. You're speeding down the highway and the feeling is superb,
   And then you hear a siren and "Pull over to the curb,"
   And when a cop who's big and tough comes walking up to you
   And asks you where the fire is that you are going to, say: *(Refrain)*

8. You go into a barbershop to get yourself a shave,
   And if you are the kind of guy who never can behave
   You ask the manicurist for a little kiss or two
   And then when you discover it's her husband shaving you, say: *(Refrain)*

*Always end A handshake and a happy greeting's mighty hard to beat,
with this   So at the risk of boring you I'm going to repeat
Verse   Remember in the future that no matter what you do
            Here's one way to get out of any mess you get into, say: *(Refrain)*

I'm Late

From Walt Disney's *Alice in Wonderland*

Words by Bob Hilliard
Music by Sammy Fain

Brightly

Cm

I'm late, I'm late for a ver-y im-por-tant date. No

C   **G7**   **C**

time to say hel-lo, good-bye, I'm late, I'm late, I'm late, I'm late and

Cm   **Em**

when I wave, I lose the time I save. My fuz-zy ears and

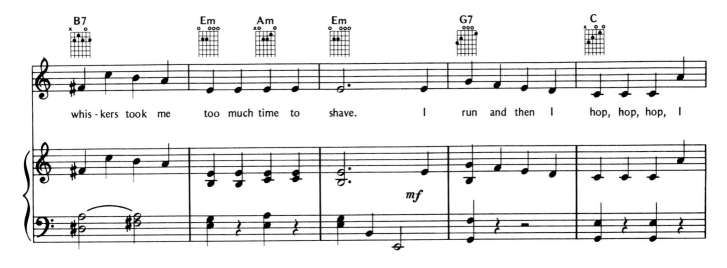

whis-kers took me too much time to shave. I run and then I hop, hop, hop, I

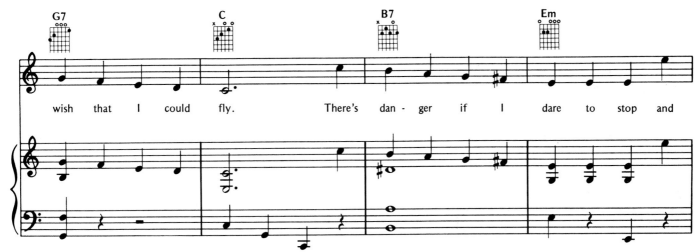

wish that I could fly. There's dan-ger if I dare to stop and

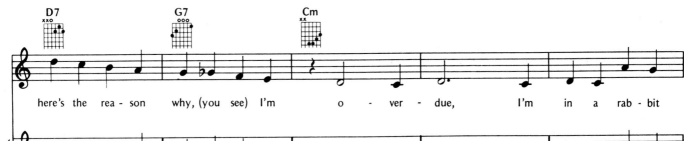

here's the rea-son why, (you see) I'm o-ver-due, I'm in a rab-bit

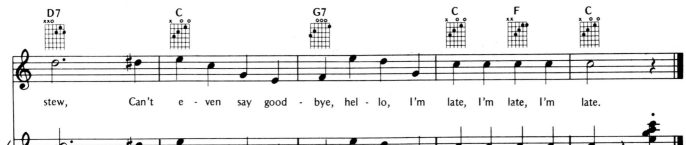

stew, Can't e-ven say good-bye, hel-lo, I'm late, I'm late, I'm late.

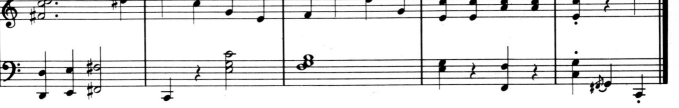

The Unbirthday Song

From Walt Disney's *Alice in Wonderland*

Words and Music by
Mack David, Al Hoffman and Jerry Livingston

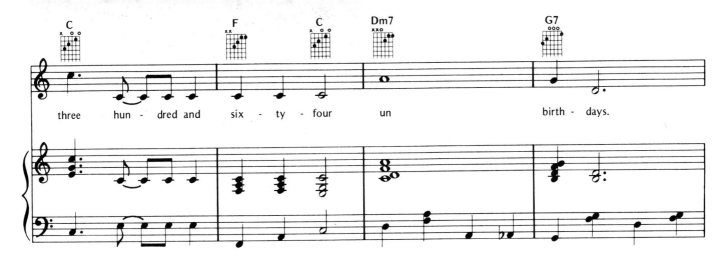

three hun - dred and six - ty - four un birth - days.

That is why we're gath - ered here to cheer. _____ A

ver - y mer - ry un - birth - day to {1. you, to you,} A
{2. me, to who?}

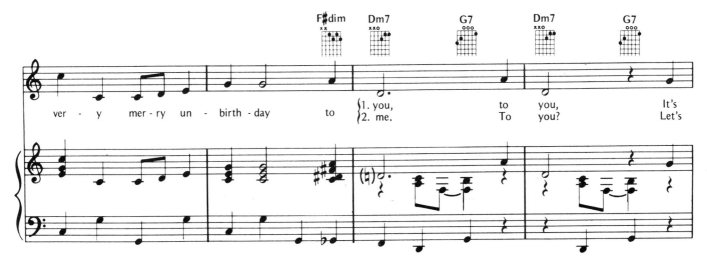

ver - y mer - ry un - birth - day to {1. you, to you, It's}
{2. me. To you? Let's}

great to drink to some-one and I guess that you will do,
all con-grat-u-late me with a pres-ent I a-gree,

A

ver-y mer-ry un-birth-day to you. ___ A

birth-day, A ver-y mer-ry un-birth-day A

ver-y mer-ry un-birth-day to me. ___

Following the Leader

From Walt Disney's *Peter Pan*

Words by Ted Sears and Winston Hibler
Music by Oliver Wallace

Gaily

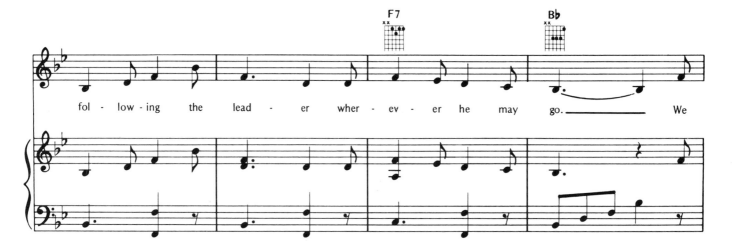

Fol-low-ing the lead - er, the lead - er, the lead - er, we're

fol - low-ing the lead - er wher-ev-er he may go. _____ We

won't be home till morn - ing, till morn - ing, till morn - ing, We

won't be home till morn - ing be - cause he told us so. Tee

dum,   Tee dee,   A tee - dle ee dō tee day.   We're
dum,   Tee dee,   A tee - dle ee dō tee day.   We

out   for fun   and this is the game we play,   Come
march a - long   and these are the words we say,   Tee

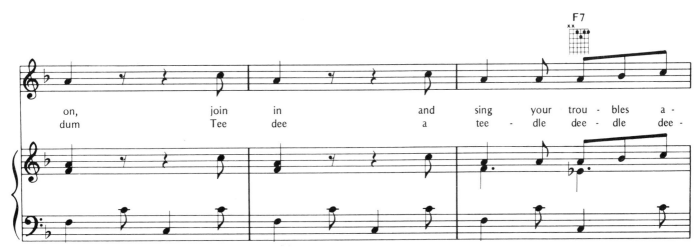

on,   join in   and sing your trou - bles a -
dum   Tee in dee   a tee - dle dee - dle dee -

way   with   a   tee - dle   ee   dum   a   tee - dle   ee   dō   tee
ay,   oh,   a   tee - dle   ee   dum   a   tee - dle   ee   dō   tee

day.   We're   day.   Oh   a

tee - dle   ee   dum   a   tee - dle   ee   dō   tee   day. _____

Never Smile at a Crocodile

From Walt Disney's *Peter Pan*

Words by Jack Lawrence
Music by Frank Churchill

Moderately slow

Ne-ver smile at a croc-o-dile, No, you can't get friend-ly with a croc-o-dile, Don't be tak-en in by his wel-come grin, He's im-ag-in-ing how well you'd fit with-in his skin. Nev-er smile at a croc-o-dile, Nev-er tip your hat and stop to talk a while {Nev-er / Don't be

96

run, Walk a - way, say "Good - night" not "Good day!")
rude, Nev - er mock, Throw a kiss, Not a rock. } Clear the aisle and nev - er smile at Mis - ter

Croc - o - dile. Croc - o - dile. You may ver - y

well be well - bred, Lots of et - i - quette in your head, But there's al - ways

some spe - cial case, time or place to for - get et - i - quette. Spoken:(F'rinstance)

The Second Star to the Right

From Walt Disney's *Peter Pan*

Words by Sammy Cahn
Music by Sammy Fain

Slowly, with expression

The sec - ond star to the right shines in the night for
The sec - ond star to the right shines with a light that's

you
rare,

to tell you that the dreams you plan
and if it's Nev - er Land you need, its

1. real - ly can come true.

2. light will lead you there.

You Can Fly! You Can Fly! You Can Fly!

From Walt Disney's *Peter Pan*

Moderately

Words by Sammy Cahn
Music by Sammy Fain

Think of the pres-ents you've brought / An-y mer-ry lit-tle thought
When there's a smile in your heart / There's no bet-ter time to start

Think of Christ-mas, think of snow, / Think of sleigh bells Here we go! Like
It's a ver-y sim-ple plan. / You can do what bird-ies can; At

rein-deer in the sky_____ / You can fly! You can
least it's worth a try_____ /

To Coda

100

Mickey Mouse March

From Walt Disney's TV Series *Mickey Mouse Club*

Words and Music by Jimmie Dodd

Mick - ey Mouse Club! Mick - ey Mouse Club!

Who's the lead - er of the club that's made for you and me!
Hey, there! Hi, there! Ho, there! You're as wel - come as can be!

M - I - C - K - E - Y M - O - U - S - E!

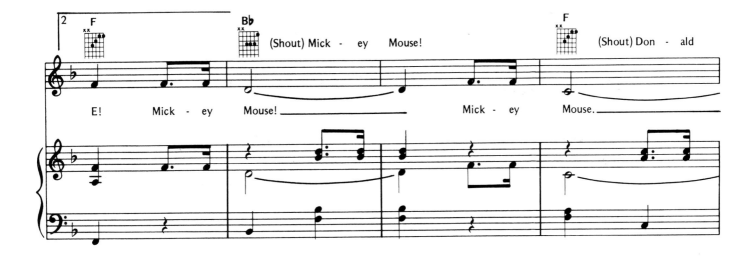

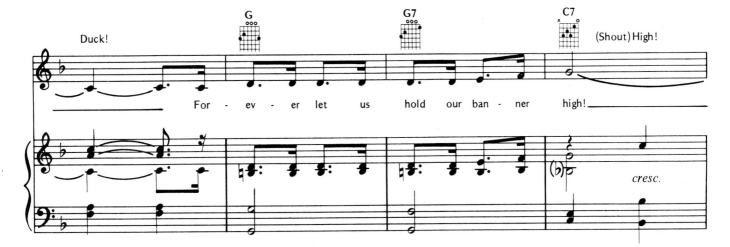

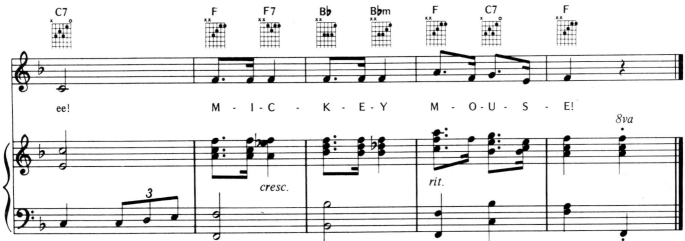

Bella Notte

From Walt Disney's *Lady and the Tramp*

Words and Music by Peggy Lee
and Sonny Burke

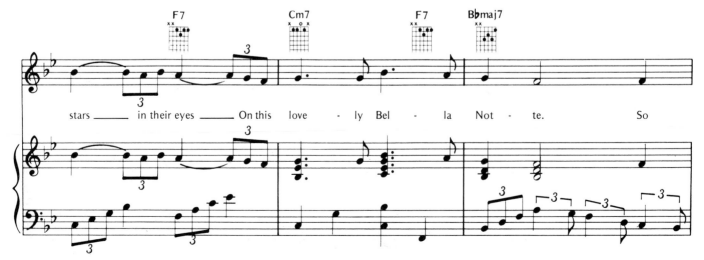

104

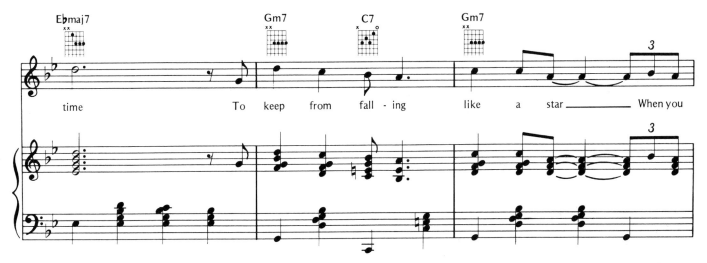
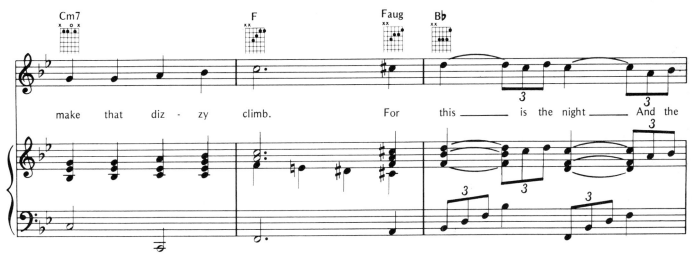

He's a Tramp

From Walt Disney's *Lady and the Tramp*

Words and Music by Peggy Lee
and Sonny Burke

Lyrics:

He's a tramp, but they love him; Breaks a new heart ev-'ry day. He's a tramp; they a-dore him And I on-ly hope he'll stay that way. He's a

tramp, he's a scoun-drel, He's a round-er, he's a cad, He's a tramp, but I love him. Yes, ev-en I have got it pret-ty bad. You can nev-er tell when

8va lower

La-La-Lu

From Walt Disney's *Lady and the Tramp*

Words and Music by Peggy Lee
and Sonny Burke

Lyrics (verse 1):
La-la-lu, la-la-lu, Oh, my lit-tle star sweep-er, I'll sweep the star-dust for you.

Lyrics (verse 2):
lu, la-la-lu, Lit-tle wan-der-ing an-gel,

La-la-lu, la-la-lu, Lit-tle soft, fluff-y

sleep- er, Here comes a pink cloud for you. ___

___ La - la - Fold up your wings for to - night. ___

___ La - la - lu, la - la - lu And may love be your

keep - er La - la - lu, la - la - lu, la - la - lu.

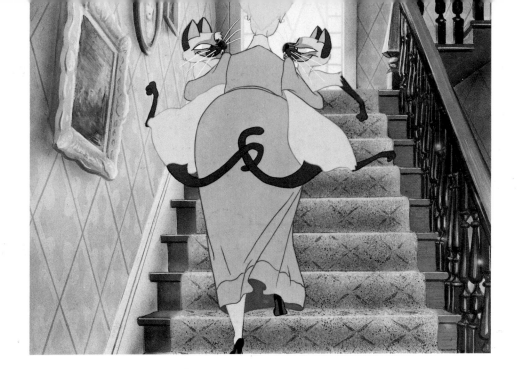

The Siamese Cat Song

From Walt Disney's *Lady and the Tramp*

Words and Music by Peggy Lee
and Sonny Burke

Dm7 G7 C

We are for-mer res-i-dents of Si-am. There {is/are} no fin-er cat than {I/we} am.

G7 C

We are Si-am-ese with ver-y dain-ty claws.

G7 Dm7

Please ob-serv-ing paws con-tain-ing dain-ty claws. Now we look-in' o-ver our new dom-i-cile.

G7 C G7 C

If we like we stay for may-be quite a while.

The Ballad of Davy Crockett

From Walt Disney's Television Production *Davy Crockett*

Words by Tom Blackburn
Music by George Bruns

Born on a moun-tain top in Ten - nes - see, Green - est state in the

Land of the Free. Raised in the woods so's he knew ev -'ry tree

Kilt him a b'ar when he was on -ly three. Da - vy, Da - vy Crock-ett,

King of the wild fron - tier! In eight - een thir - teen the Creeks up - rose, add - in' red - skin ar - rows to the coun - try's woes. Now In - jun fight - in' is some - thin' he knows so he shoul - ders his ri - fle an' off he goes.

Chorus

Da - vy, Da - vy Crock - ett, the man who don't know fear!

Wringle Wrangle
(A Pretty Woman's Love)

From Walt Disney's *Westward Ho the Wagons!*

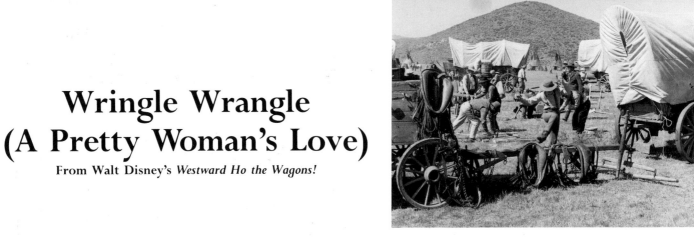

Words and Music by Stan Jones

Lively

Oh   Oh   Wrin - gle, wran - gle jing - a - jong jan - gle

(whistle) Hey! *(slap leg)* A might-y fine horse I'm in love of course 'cause I got me a pret-ty wo-man's

love.   Oh love.   With a dol-lars worth of beans, a new pair of jeans, got a

Once Upon a Dream

(Based on the *Sleeping Beauty* Theme)
From Walt Disney's *Sleeping Beauty*

Words and Adaptation of Music by
Sammy Fain and Jack Lawrence

I know you! I walked with you once up-on a dream. I know you! The gleam in your eyes is so fa-mil-iar a gleam. Yet, I

Let's Get Together

From Walt Disney's *The Parent Trap*

Words and Music by Richard M. Sherman
and Robert B. Sherman

geth-er._____ Oh!_____ Oh, I real-ly
geth-er._____

think you're swell__ Uh huh, we real-ly ring the bell. Ooh_____ee, and if you

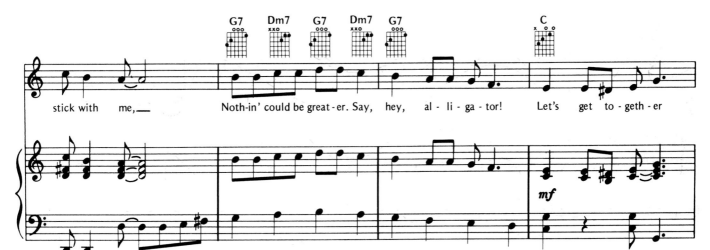

stick with me,___ Noth-in' could be great-er. Say, hey, al-li-ga-tor! Let's get to-geth-er

Yea, yea yea!__ Two is twice as nice as one.__ Let's get to-geth-er.

Right __ a - way, __ We'll be hav - in' twice the fun, __ And you can

al - ways count on me, A groov - y two - some we will

be. Let's get to - geth - er. _____ Yea, yea, yea! __

Toyland March

From Walt Disney's
Babes in Toyland

Words by Mel Leven
Music by George Bruns
Adapted from a Victor Herbert Melody

Toy - land, toy - land, Dear lit - tle girl and boy land, While you dwell with -
Toy - land, toy - land, We're on our way to toy - land, Don't know when we'll

in it You are ev - er hap - py there. Child - hood's toy - land, Won - der - ful world of
get there, But we know there's fun in store. Toy - land, toy - land, Won - der - ful girl and

joy land, Would - n't it be fine if we could stay there for - ev - er more.
boy land, Once you leave its bor - ders you can nev - er re - turn a - gain.

Cruella de Ville

From Walt Disney's *101 Dalmatians*

Words and Music by Mel Leven

Slow Blues

Lyrics:

Cru-el-la de Ville,— Cru-el-la de Ville,— if she does-n't scare you no
curl of her lips,— the ice in her stare; all in-no-cent chil-dren had

e-vil thing will.— To see her is to take a sud-den chill,— Cru-el-la, Cru-el-la de
bet-ter be-ware.— She's like a spi-der wait-ing for the kill,— Cru-

Ville. The el-la, Cru-el-la de Ville. At first you think Cru-el-la is the

dev-il,_____ but af-ter time has wore a-way the shock, you come to re-a-lize__ you've

seen her kind of eyes__ watch-ing you from un-der-neath a rock. This

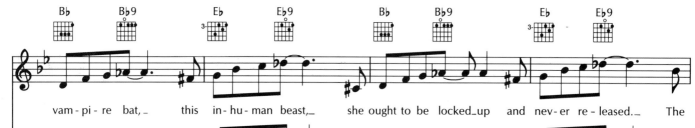

vam-pi-re bat,__ this in-hu-man beast,__ she ought to be locked_up and nev-er re-leased.__ The

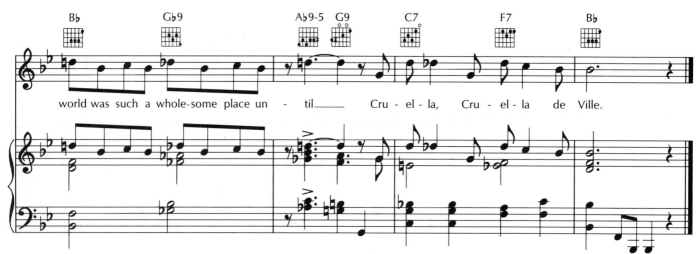

world was such a whole-some place un-til_____ Cru-el-la, Cru-el-la de Ville.

Chim Chim Cher-ee

From Walt Disney's *Mary Poppins*

Words and Music by Richard M. Sherman
and Robert B. Sherman

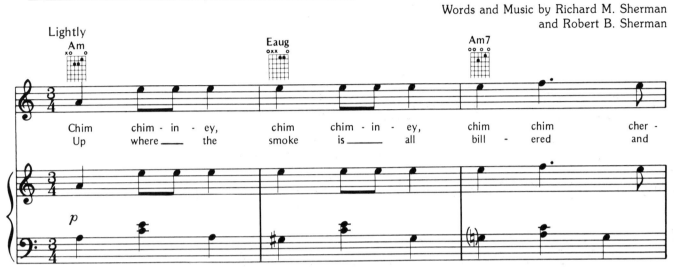

chim chim-in-ey, chim chim cher-oo! Good
day _____ nor 'ard-ly no night,

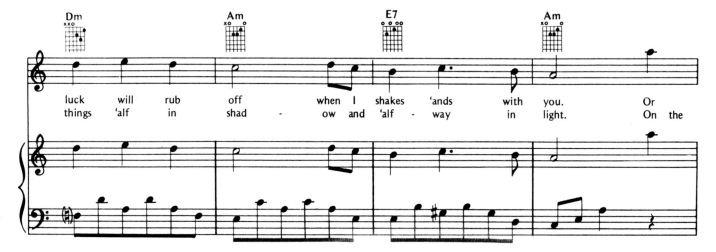

luck will rub off when I shakes 'ands with you. Or
things 'alf in shad-ow and 'alf-way in light. On the

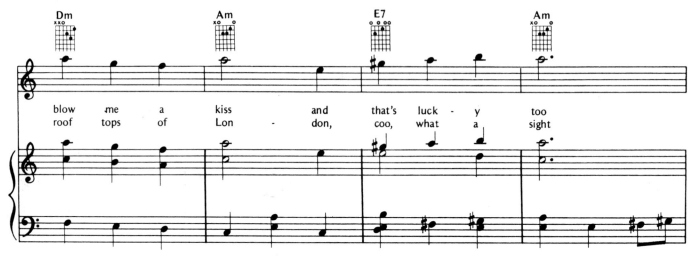

blow me a kiss and that's luck-y too
roof tops of Lon-don, coo, what a sight

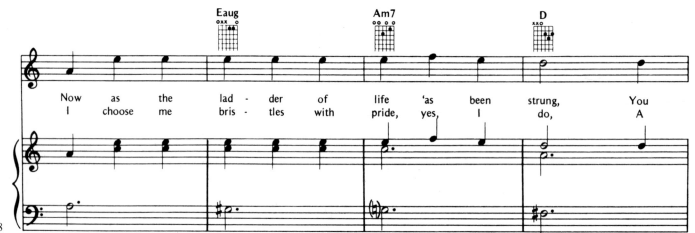

Now as the lad-der of life 'as been strung, You
I choose me bris-tles with pride, yes, I do, A

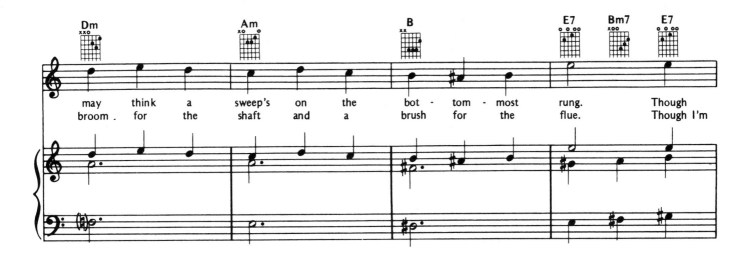

may think a sweep's on the bot - tom - most rung. Though
broom . for the shaft and a brush for the flue. Though I'm

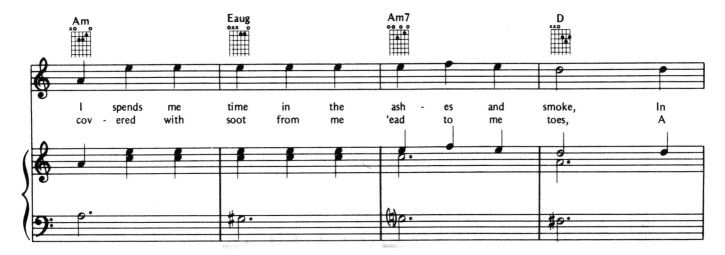

I spends me time in the ash - es and smoke, In
cov - ered with soot from me 'ead to me toes, A

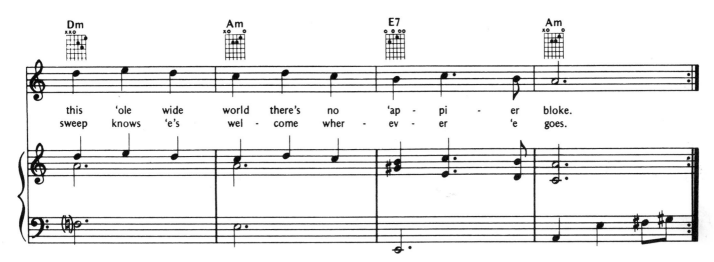

this 'ole wide world there's no 'ap - pi - er bloke.
sweep knows 'e's wel - come wher - ev - er 'e goes.

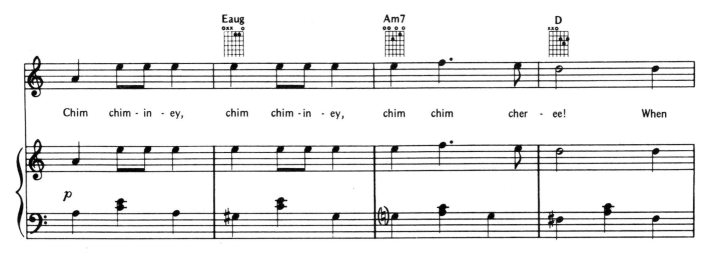

Chim chim - in - ey, chim chim - in - ey, chim chim cher - ee! When

Feed the Birds
(Tuppence a Bag)

From Walt Disney's *Mary Poppins*

Words and Music by Richard M. Sherman
and Robert B. Sherman

Feed ____ the birds, tup-pence ____ a bag,

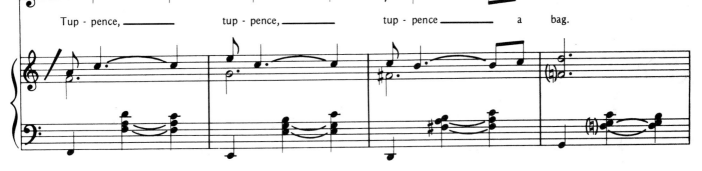

Tup-pence, ____ tup-pence, ____ tup-pence ____ a bag.

"Feed ____ the birds," that's what she cries

131

Slightly faster

While o - ver - head her birds fill the skies. All a-

round the ca - the - dral the saints and a - post - les Look

down as she sells her wares._____ Al-

though you can't see it, you know they are smil - ing Each

132

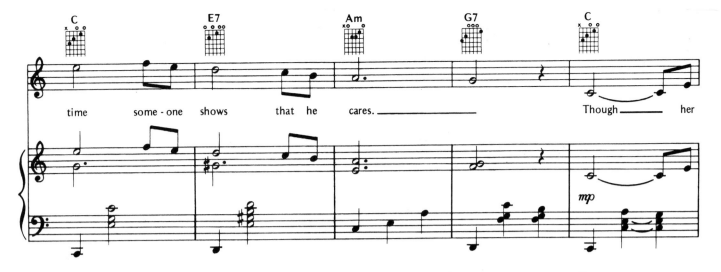

time some-one shows that he cares._____ Though_____ her

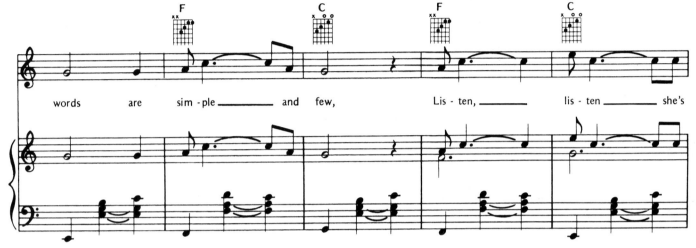

words are sim-ple_____ and few, Lis-ten,_____ lis-ten_____ she's

cal-ling to you. "Feed_____ the birds, tup-pence_____ a

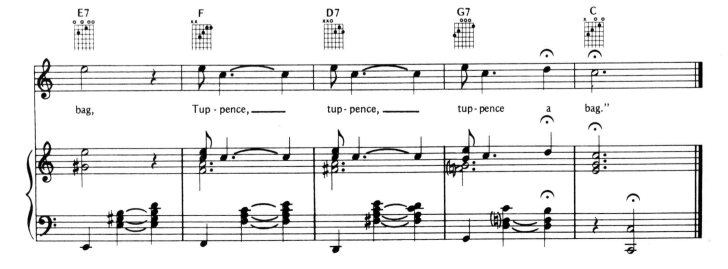

bag, Tup-pence,_____ tup-pence,_____ tup-pence a bag."

I Love to Laugh

From Walt Disney's *Mary Poppins*

Words and Music by Richard M. Sherman
and Robert B. Sherman

I love to laugh, Ha! Ha! Ha! Ha!

Loud and long and clear. _____ I love to

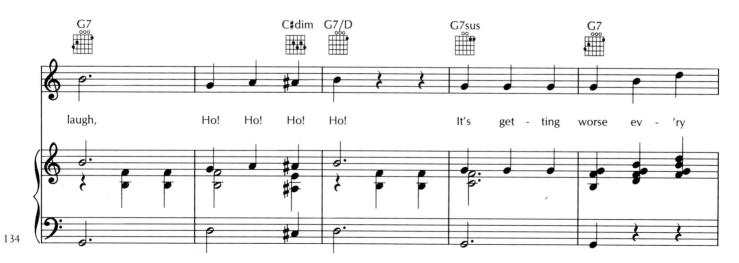

laugh, Ho! Ho! Ho! Ho! It's get-ting worse ev-'ry

year. _____ The more I laugh, Ha! Ha! Ha!

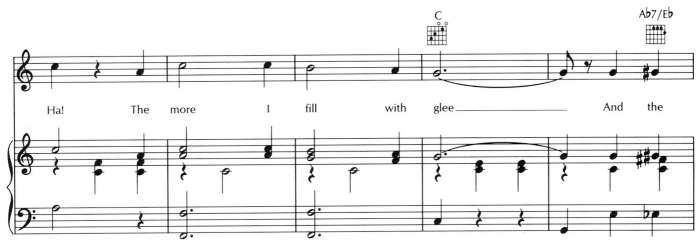

Ha! The more I fill with glee_____ And the

more the glee, He! He! He! He! The

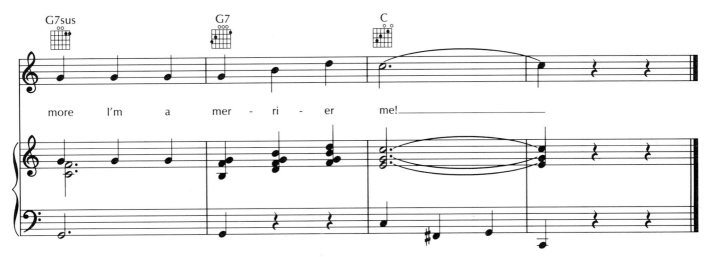

more I'm a mer - ri - er me!_____

Let's Go
Fly a Kite

From Walt Disney's *Mary Poppins*

Words and Music by Richard M. Sherman
and Robert B. Sherman

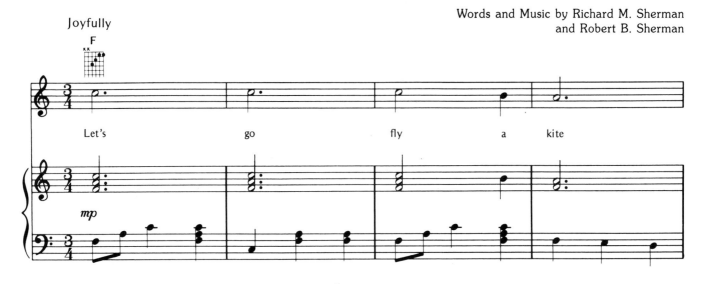

Joyfully

Let's go fly a kite

up to the high - est height!

Let's go fly a kite and

136

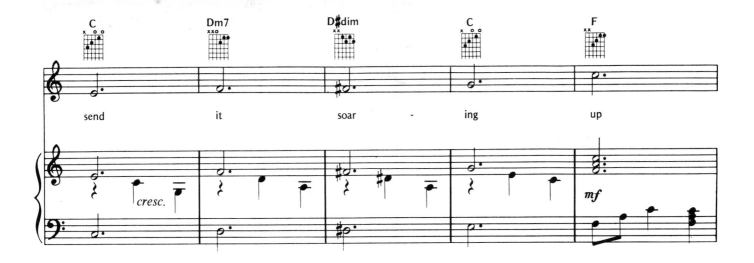

send it soar - ing up

through the at - mos - phere, Up where the

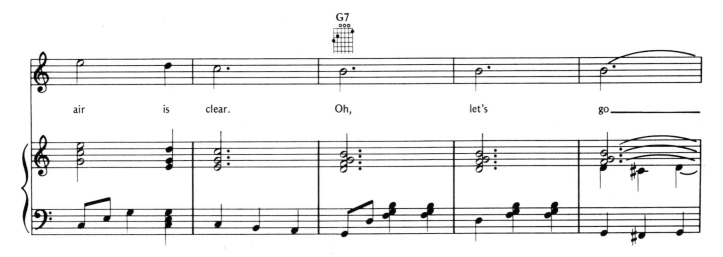

air is clear. Oh, let's go_____

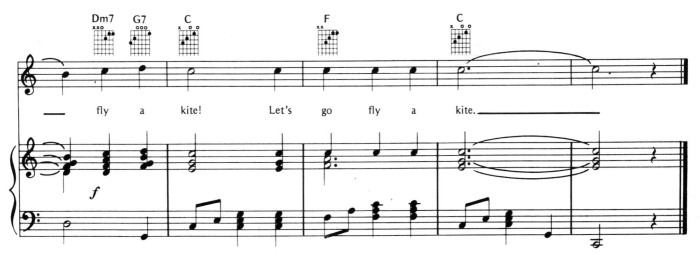

___ fly a kite! Let's go fly a kite.___

A Spoonful of Sugar

From Walt Disney's *Mary Poppins*

Words and Music by Richard M. Sherman
and Robert B. Sherman

139

snap the job's a game;_____ And ev-'ry task you un-der-
bits of twine and twig. _____ Though quite in-tent in his pur-

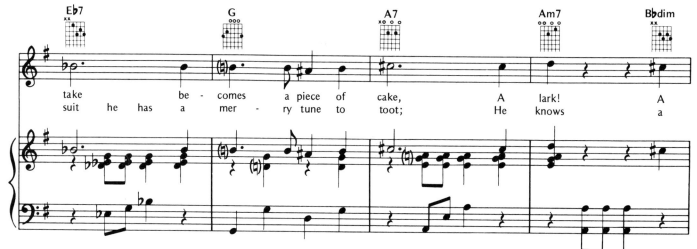

take be-comes a piece of cake, A lark! A
suit he has a mer-ry tune to toot; He knows a

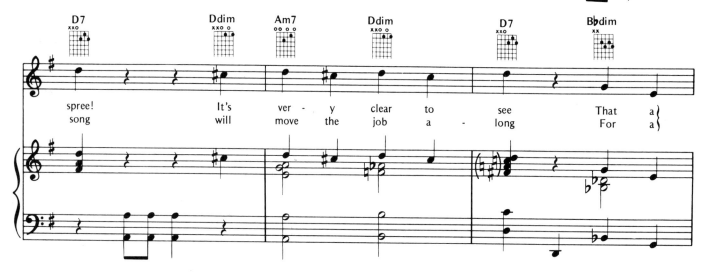

spree! It's ver-y clear to see That a
song will move the job a-long For a

spoon-ful of su-gar helps the med-i-cine go

141

Step In Time

From Walt Disney's *Mary Poppins*

Words and Music by Richard M. Sherman
and Robert B. Sherman

Spirited

Kick your knees up,
Spin a-bout and

step in time! Kick your knees up, step in time! Nev-er need a rea-son, nev-er need a rhyme,
step in time! Spin a-bout and step in time! Nev-er need a rea-son, nev-er need a rhyme,

Kick your knees up, step in time! Link your el-bows, step in time! Link your el-bows,
Spin a-bout and step in time! 'Round the chim-ney, step in time! 'Round the chim-ney,

step in time! Nev-er need a rea-son, nev-er need a rhyme, Link your el-bows, step in time!
step in time! Nev-er need a rea-son, nev-er need a rhyme, 'Round the chim-ney, step in time!

Flap like a bird - ie,
Step in time,

step in time! Flap like a bird-ie, step in time! Nev-er need a rea-son, nev-er need a rhyme,
step in time, Step in time, step in time! Nev-er need a rea-son, nev-er need a rhyme, When you

Flap like a bird - ie, step in time! step in time, you step in time!

Supercalifragilisticexpialidocious

From Walt Disney's *Mary Poppins*

Words and Music by Richard M. Sherman
and Robert B. Sherman

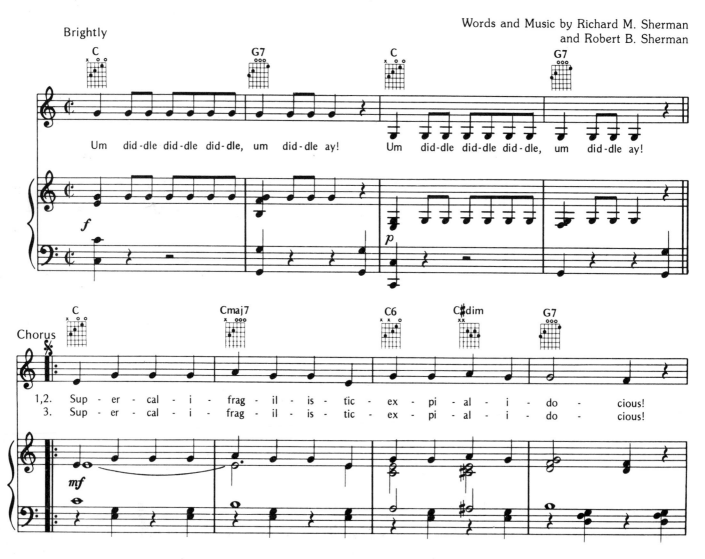

Brightly

C G7 C G7

Um did-dle did-dle did-dle, um did-dle ay! Um did-dle did-dle did-dle, um did-dle ay!

Chorus

C Cmaj7 C6 C#dim G7

1,2. Sup - er - cal - i - frag - il - is - tic - ex - pi - al - i - do - cious!
3. Sup - er - cal - i - frag - il - is - tic - ex - pi - al - i - do - cious!

It's a Small World

Theme from the Disneyland and Walt Disney
World Attraction, *It's a Small World*

Words and Music by Richard M. Sherman
and Robert B. Sherman

It's a world of laugh-ter, a world of tears; it's a
just one moon and one gold-en sun

world of hopes and a world of fears. There's so
smile means friend - ship to ev - 'ry one, Though the

much that we share that it's time we're a - ware. It's a
moun - tains di - vide that and the o - ceans are wide, It's a

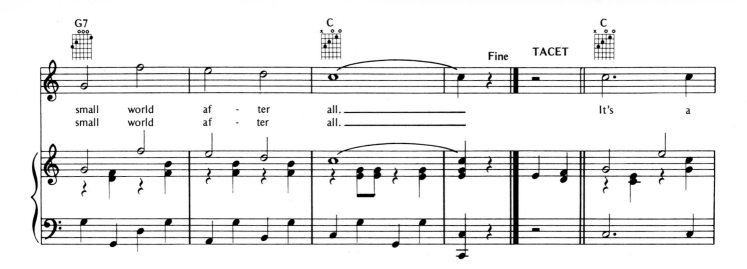

small world af - ter all. _____ Fine TACET It's a
small world af - ter all. _____ It's a

small world af - ter all, It's a small world

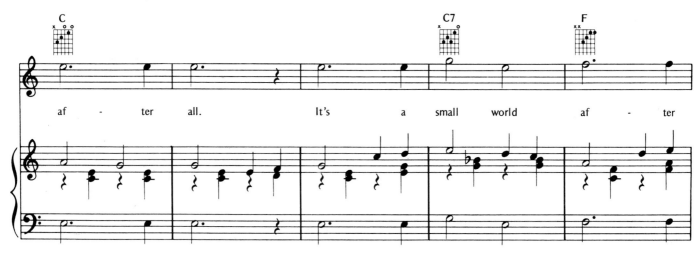

af - ter all. It's a small world af - ter

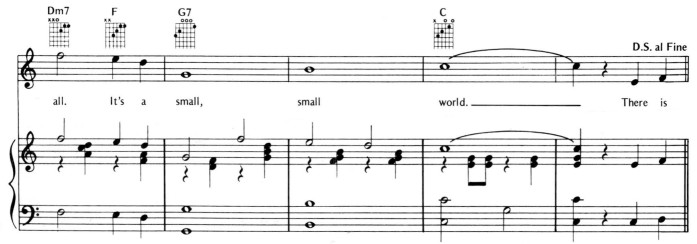

all. It's a small, small world. _____ There is

148

Winnie the Pooh

From Walt Disney's
Winnie the Pooh and the Honey Tree

Words and Music by Richard M. Sherman
and Robert B. Sherman

and there's Owl, but most of all Win-nie the Pooh!

Win-nie the Pooh, Win-nie the Pooh, tub-by lit-tle cub-by all

stuffed with fluff, He's Win-nie the Pooh, Win-nie the Pooh;

wil-ly, nil-ly, sil-ly ole bear. bear.

The Bare Necessities

From Walt Disney's *The Jungle Book*

Words and Music by Terry Gilkyson

Brightly

Look for the bare ne-ces-si-ties, the sim-ple bare ne-

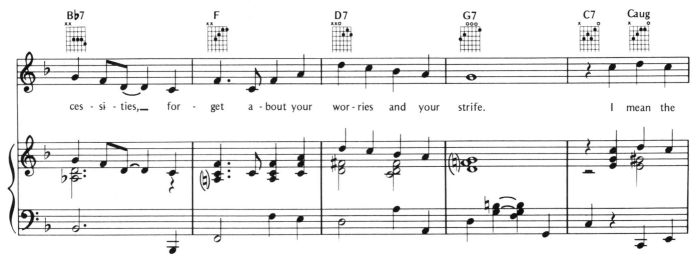

ces-si-ties,__ for-get a-bout your wor-ries and your strife. I mean the

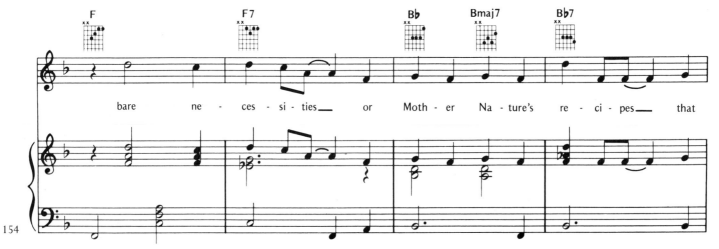

bare ne-ces-si-ties__ or Moth-er Na-ture's re-ci-pes__ that

154

bring the bare ne - ces - si - ties — of life _____ Wher - ev - er I wan - der, —

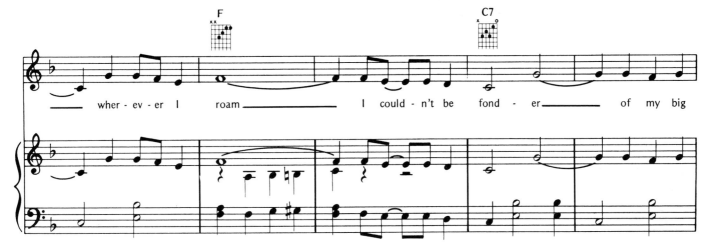

—— wher - ev - er I roam _____ I could - n't be fond - er _____ of my big

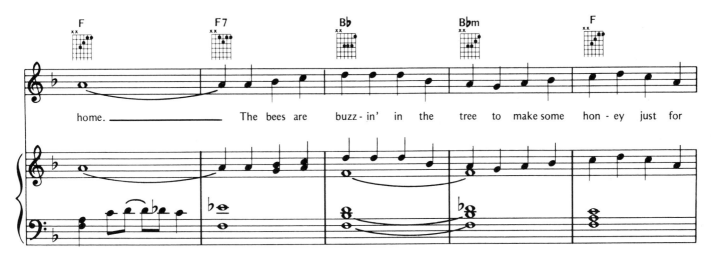

home. _____ The bees are buzz - in' in the tree to make some hon - ey just for

me, The bare ne - cess - si - ties of life will come to you. _____

I Wan'na Be
Like You
(The Monkey Song)

From Walt Disney's *The Jungle Book*

Words and Music by Richard M. Sherman
and Robert B. Sherman

Now I'm the king of the swing-ers, the jun-gle V. I. P.
try to kid me, man-cub, and don't get in a stew

I've reached the top and had to stop and that's what's both-er-in' me. I wan-na be a man
what I de-sire is man's red fire, so I can be like you. Give me the sec-ret

man - cub, And stroll right in - to town,
and
man - cub, Just clue me what to do,
and give

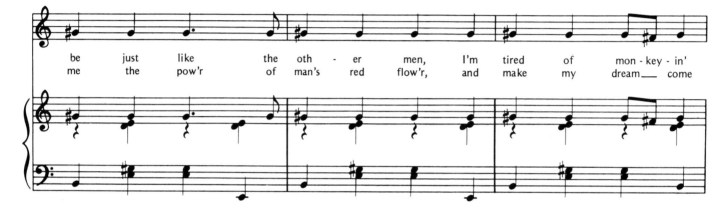

be just like the oth - er men, I'm tired of mon - key - in'
me the pow'r of man's red flow'r, and make my dream__ come

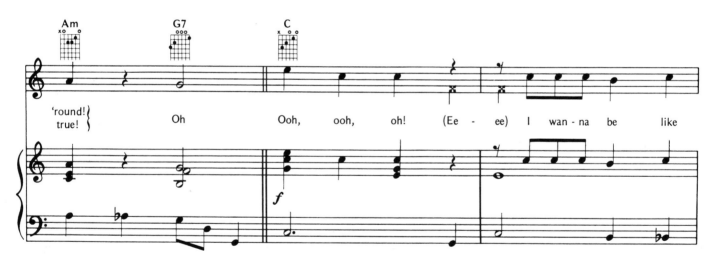

'round!}
true! }
Oh Ooh, ooh, oh! (Ee - ee) I wan - na be like

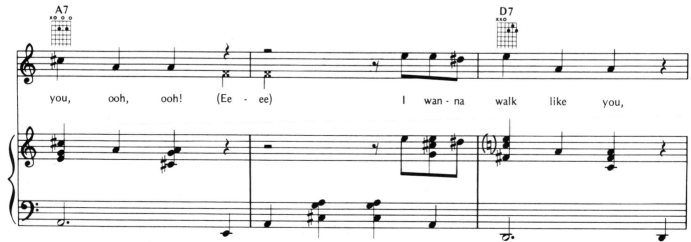

you, ooh, ooh! (Ee - ee) I wan - na walk like you,

158

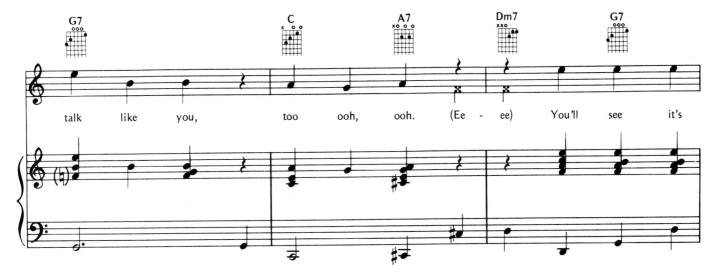

talk like you, too ooh, ooh. (Ee - ee) You'll see it's

true, ooh, ooh! (Ee - ee) An ape like me, ee, ee (ooh -

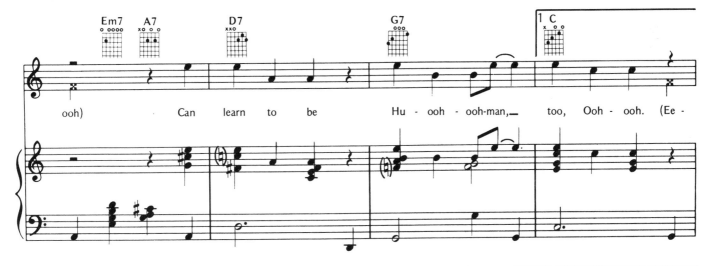

ooh) Can learn to be Hu - ooh - ooh-man,— too, Ooh - ooh. (Ee -

ee) Don't too, Ooh - ooh. (Ee - ee)

Fortuosity

From Walt Disney's *The Happiest Millionaire*

Words and Music by Richard M. Sherman
and Robert B. Sherman

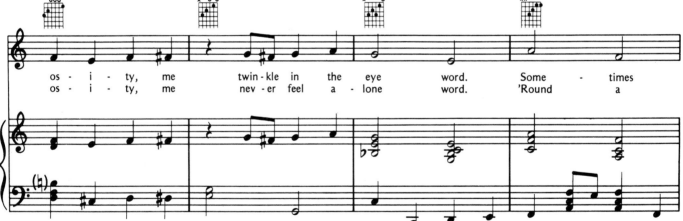

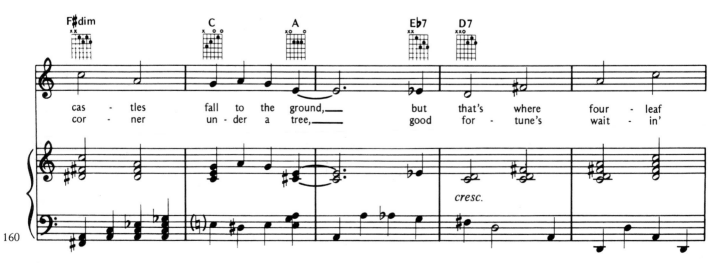

For - tu - os - i - ty, That's me by word. For - tu -
For - tu - os - i - ty, That's me own word. For - tu -

os - i - ty, me twin - kle in the eye word. Some - times
os - i - ty, me nev - er feel a - lone word. 'Round a

cas - tles fall to the ground,___ but that's where four - leaf
cor - ner un - der a tree,___ good for - tune's wait - in'

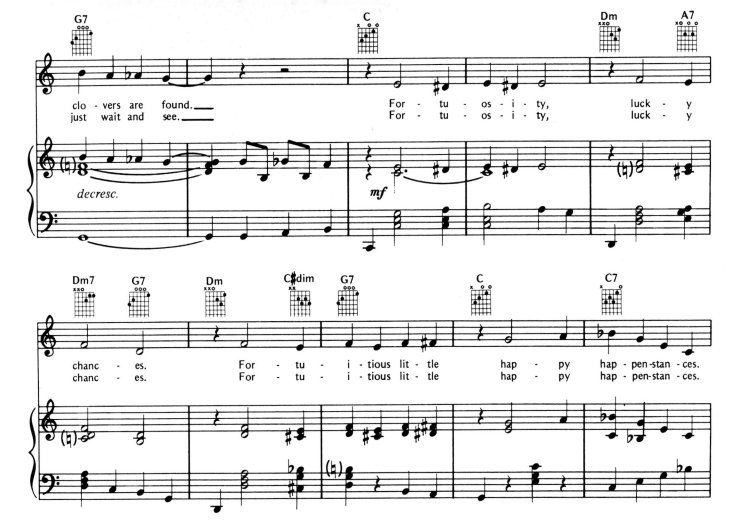

clo - vers are found.____
just wait and see.____
For - tu - os - i - ty, luck - y
For - tu - os - i - ty, luck - y

decresc.

mf

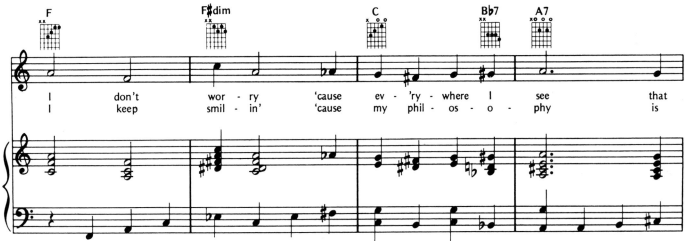

chanc - es. For - tu - i - tious lit - tle hap - py hap - pen-stan - ces.
chanc - es. For - tu - i - tious lit - tle hap - py hap - pen-stan - ces.

I don't wor - ry 'cause ev - 'ry - where I see that
I keep smil - in' 'cause my phil - os - o - phy is

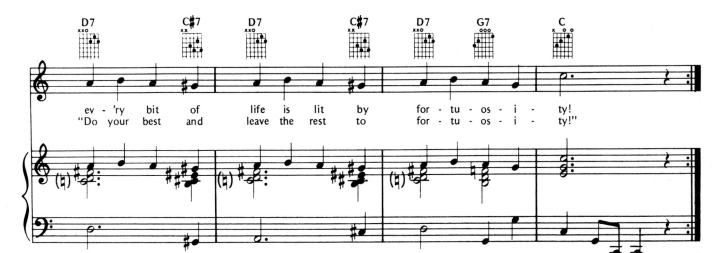

ev - 'ry bit of life is lit by for - tu - os - i - ty!
"Do your best and leave the rest to for - tu - os - i - ty!"

Yo, Ho
(A Pirate's Life for Me)

From Walt Disney's *Disneyland*

Words by Xavier Atencio
Music by George Bruns

In a robust manner

Yo ho, yo ho, a pi - rate's life for me. We
Yo ho, yo ho, a pi - rate's life for me. We
Yo ho, yo ho, a pi - rate's life for me. We

pil - lage, plun - der, we ri - fle and loot. Drink up me 'eart - ies, yo ho. We
ex - tort and pil - fer, we filch and sack. Drink up me 'eart - ies, yo ho. Ma -
kin - dle and char and in - flame and ig - nite. Drink up me 'eart - ies, yo ho. We

kid - nap and rav - age and don't give a hoot. Drink up me 'eart - ies, yo ho.
raud and em - bez - zle and e - ven high - jack. Drink up me 'eart - ies, yo ho.
burn up the cit - y, we're real - ly a fright. Drink

162

up   me 'eart - ies,   yo ho.   We're ras - cals   and   scoun - drels, we're

vil - lians   and   knaves.   Drink   up   me 'eart - ies,   yo ho.   We're

dev - ils   and   black sheep, we're   real - ly   bad eggs.   Drink   up   me 'eart - ies,   yo

ho.   Yo ho,   yo ho,   a   pi - rate's   life   for   me.

sfz

The Wonderful Thing about Tiggers

From Walt Disney's *Winnie the Pooh and the Blustery Day*

Words and Music by Richard M. Sherman
and Robert B. Sherman

Ev'rybody Wants to Be a Cat

From Walt Disney's *The Aristocats*

Words and Music by Floyd Huddleston
and Al Rinker

Ev-'ry-bod-y wants to be a cat, be-cause a cat's the on-ly cat who knows where it's at! Ev-'ry-bod-y pick-in' up on the fe-line beat, 'cause ev-'ry-thing else is ob-so-lete. Be-ware of a square when he of-fers to share his

167

milk to sip!__ If it has-n't been tried,__ I sug-gest you pro-vide__ your own cat-nip.__ I've heard some corn-y birds who tried to sing, But still a cat's the on-ly cat who knows how to swing!__ A purr be-tween two fur-ry friends may be old hat,__ But ev-'ry-bod-y wants to be a cat!__ be a cat!__

To next strain

FINE

F♯m7 B7 F♯m7 B7 E C7 F♯m B7
Come on, scat cat, turn me on,_ I'll take my horn and my best tone,_ Then blow a lit - tle soul in - to the
Emaj7 Amaj7 Emaj7 Gm7 C7 Gm7 C7
tune. Let's take it to an-oth-er key,_ Mod - u-late, then wait for me,_ I'll
Fmaj7 Gm Fmaj7 A♭m7 D♭7
take a few ad libs and pret - ty soon The oth - er cats will all com-mence_
A♭m7 D♭7 Am7 D7 Am7 Am7-5 F♯m7 B7
D.C. al Fine
con - gre-gat - ing on the fence,_be - neath the al - ley's on-ly light,_where ev - 'ry night is out of sight!

Scales and Arpeggios

From Walt Disney's *The Aristocats*

Words and Music by Richard M. Sherman
and Robert B. Sherman

Ev -'ry tru -ly cul-tured mu -sic stu - dent knows, You must learn your scales and your ar - peg - gi - os.

Bring the mu - sic ring - ing from your chest and not your nose, While you sing your scales and your ar -

peg - gi - os. Do mi so do do so mi do If you're faith - ful to your dai - ly

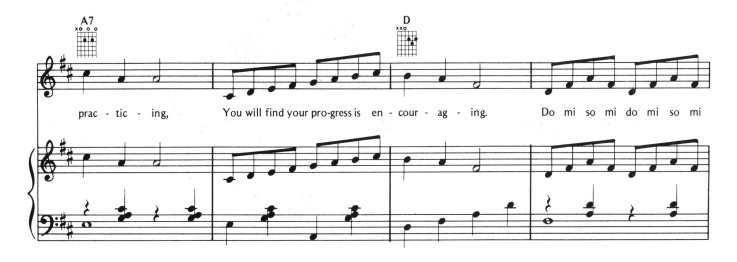

prac - tic - ing, You will find your pro-gress is en - cour - ag - ing. Do mi so mi do mi so mi

fa la so it goes, When you do the scales and your ar - peg - gi - os.

Do mi so do do so mi do do mi so do do so mi do Train your-self to draw a line that's

straight and true, Then your brush will do just what you want it to.

171

These Are the Best Times

From Walt Disney Productions' *Superdad*

Words and Music by Shane Tatum

Tenderly

These are the best times— the mo-ments we can't let slip a-
But once in a life time— a min-ute like this is ours— to

way life's lit-tle game— we play for liv-ing from day to
share re-mem-ber these mo - ments well

day.— mo-ments like these are rare as dreams and

Love

From Walt Disney Productions' *Robin Hood*

Words by Floyd Huddleston
Music by George Bruns

flee. _____ Once we watched a la - zy world go

by. Now the days seem to fly. _____

Life is brief, but when it's gone, _____ Love goes

on and on. _____ on. _____

Oo-De-Lally

From Walt Disney Productions' *Robin Hood*

Words and Music by Roger Miller

Moderately

Rob-in Hood and Lit-tle John walk-in' thru the for-est, Laugh-in' back and forth at what the
Rob-in Hood and Lit-tle John run-nin' thru the for-est, Jump-in' fen-ces dodg-in' trees and

oth-er 'un has to say. Re-min-isc-in' this 'n that 'n
try-in' to get a-way. Con-tem-pla-tin' noth-in' but es-

hav-in' such a good time. } Oo-de-lal-ly, Hoo-de-lal-ly, Gol-ly what a day!
cape and fin-'ly makin' it.

Sweet Surrender

From Walt Disney Productions' *The Bears and I*

Words and Music by John Denver

I'd like to do _____ with my life. _____ There's

noth-in' _____ be - hind me and _____ noth-in' _____ that ties me to _____

_____ some-thing that might have been _____ true yes - ter - day. _____ To -

mor - row _____ is o - pen, _____ right now seems _____ to be

more than e - nough,____ just ___ be here to - day,

and he don't know what____ the fu - ture is hold - in' in

store. I don't know where I'm go - in', I'm not sure where I've been.__

_____ There's a spir - it that guides me,__ a

light that shines for me,___ my life is worth the liv - in', I don't

need to see___ the end._____

Sweet,_____ sweet sur - ren - der,_____ live,_____

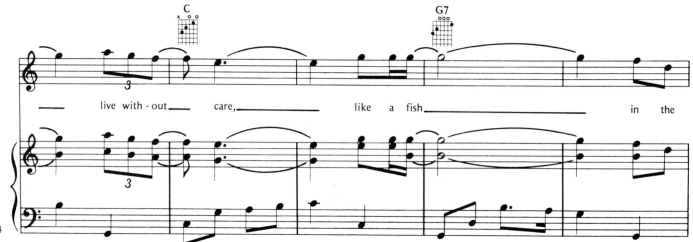

—— live with - out___ care,_____ like a fish_____ in the

wa - ter, _____ like a bird _____ in the air. _____

Sweet _____ sur - ren - der, _____ live, _____ live with-out_

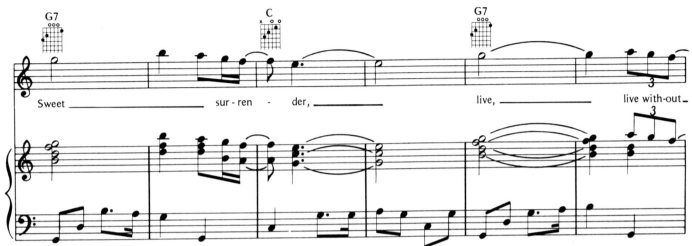

___ care, _____ like a fish _____ in the wa - ter, _____ like a bird_

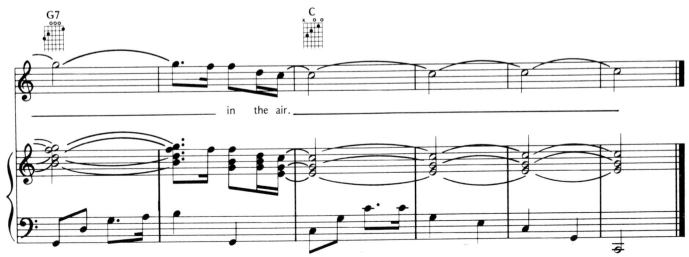

in the air. _____

Someone's Waiting for You

From Walt Disney Productions' *The Rescuers*

Words by Carol Connors and Ayn Robbins
Music by Sammy Fain

Ev - 'ry child has man - y wish - es that they wish when they're a - lone. Faith can work just like mag - ic; noth - ing chang - es when you're grown. Be brave lit - tle one Make a wish for each sad lit - tle tear

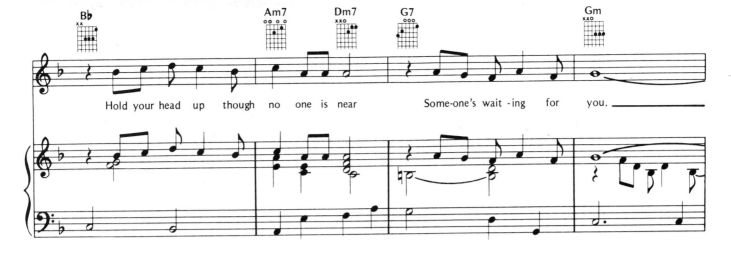

Hold your head up though no one is near   Some-one's wait-ing for you. _____

_____ Don't cry lit - tle one   There'll be a smile where a   frown used to be

You'll be part of the love that you see   Some - one's wait - ing for   you. _____

_____ Al - ways keep a lit - tle prayer in your pock - et   and you're sure to see the

light.   Soon there'll be joy and hap - pi - ness and your lit - tle world will be

bright.   Have faith lit - tle one   'til your hopes and your wish - es come true

You must try to be brave lit - tle one_____   Some - one's wait - ing

to love you._____

8va lower

Candle
on the Water

From Walt Disney Productions' *Pete's Dragon*

Words and Music by Al Kasha
and Joel Hirschhorn

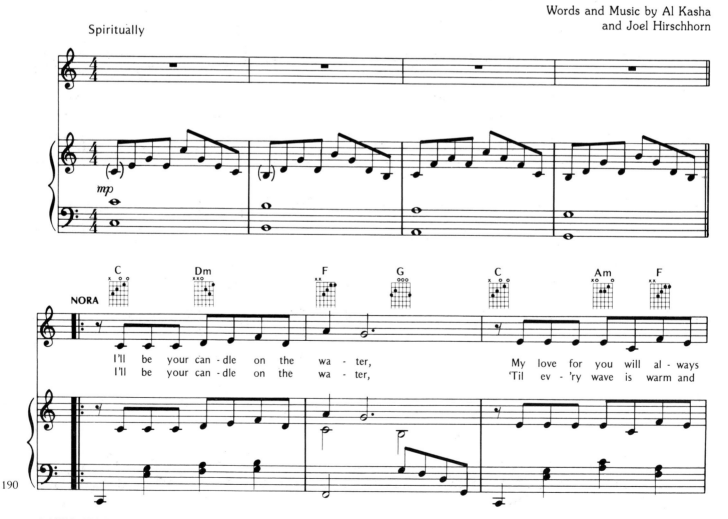

Spiritually

NORA

I'll be your can-dle on the wa - ter,   My love for you will al - ways
I'll be your can-dle on the wa - ter,   'Til ev - 'ry wave is warm and

190

burn.   I know you're lost   and drift-ing,   But the clouds are lift-ing,
bright.   My soul is   there   be-side you,   Let this can-dle guide you

don't give up you have some-where to   turn.
soon, you'll see a gold-en stream of   light.

A cold and friend-less tide has found   you,   don't let the storm-y dark-ness

pull you down.   I'll paint a ray of hope a-round   you,

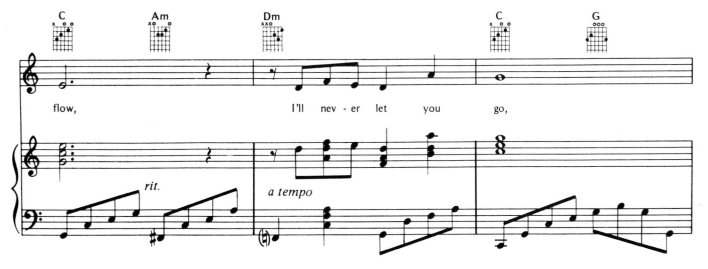

flow,   I'll nev - er let you   go,

rit.   *a tempo*

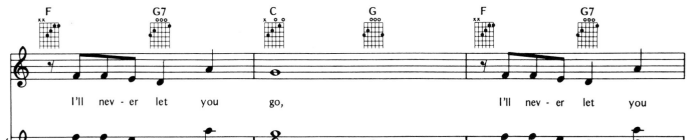

I'll nev - er let you   go,   I'll nev - er let you

go.

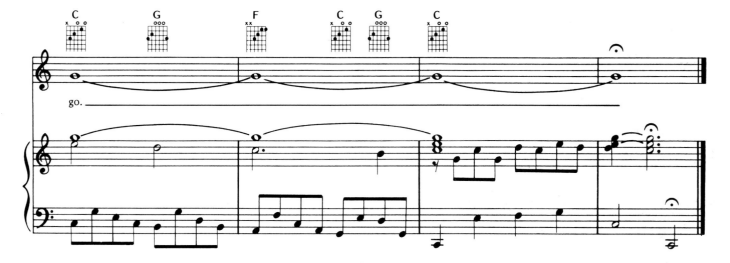

193

It's Not Easy

From Walt Disney Productions' *Pete's Dragon*

Words and Music by Al Kasha
and Joel Hirschhorn

195

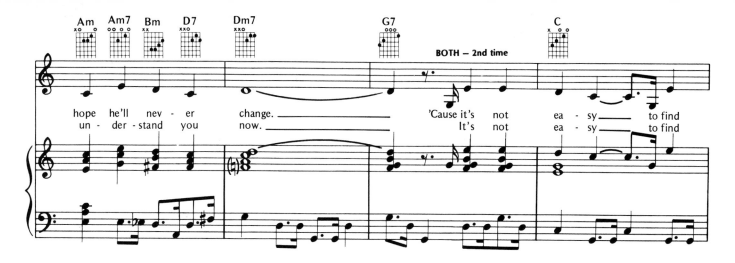

hope he'll nev - er change. _____ 'Cause it's not ea - sy _____ to find
un - der - stand you now. _____ It's not ea - sy _____ to find

BOTH — 2nd time

some - one who cares, ____ it's not ea - sy _____ to find mag - ic in pairs, I'm glad I
some - one who cares, ____ it's not ea - sy _____ to find mag - ic in pairs, now that you

NORA
1st time

PETE
1st time
NORA
2nd time

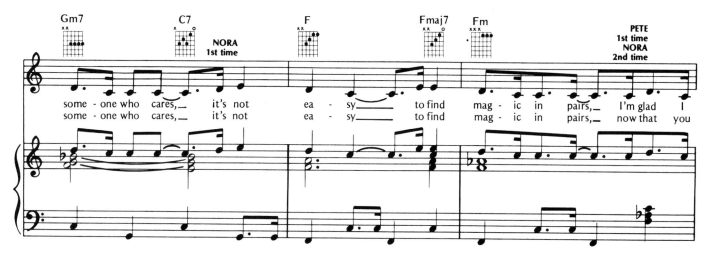

found him, I love him, I won't let him get a - way.
have him, _____ hold him, trea - sure him from day to day.

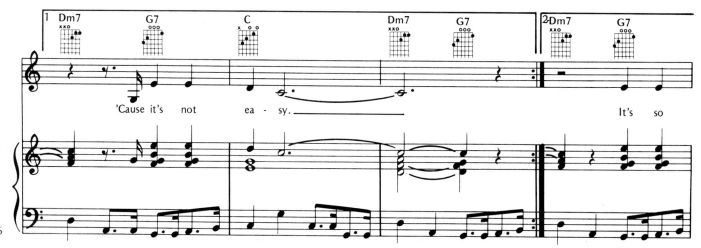

1 'Cause it's not ea - sy. _____

2 It's so

197

NORA ... PETE

work as a team__ you've got to tend it, fan it, that's what I plan to do __ oh I had

one friend by my side ____ now I have two _____ him and you__

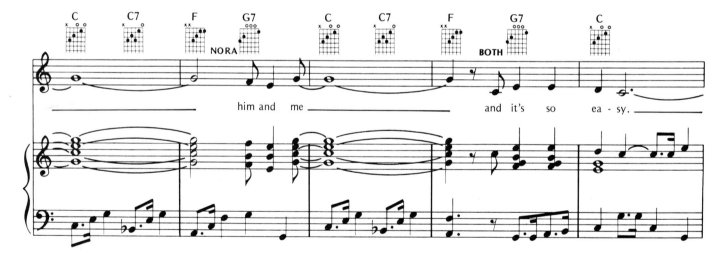

NORA ... BOTH

_____ him and me _____ and it's so ea-sy. _____

Disco
Mickey Mouse

From Walt Disney Productions' *Mickey Mouse Disco*

Words and Music by Tom Worrall

Lyrics:

He's a mov-ie star. ___
mach-o guy ___

The la-dies say he's sweet. ___ Well, his
with Clark Ga-ble ears. ___ When his

bod-y's got ___ the mo-tion and the rhy-thm's in ___ his feet. ___
bod-y's set ___ in mo-tion, the la-dies cry a thou-sand tears. ___

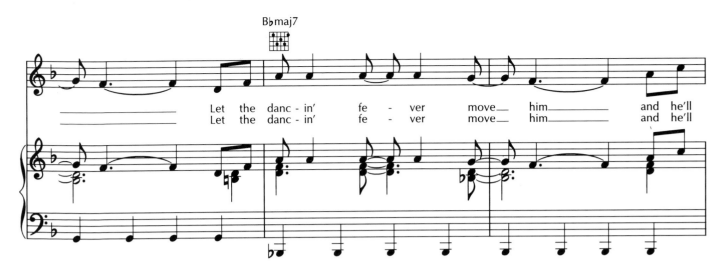

Disco
Mickey Mouse

From Walt Disney Productions' *Mickey Mouse Disco*

Words and Music by Tom Worrall

He's a mov - ie star. ____
mach - o guy ____

The la - dies say he's sweet. ____
with Clark Ga - ble ears. ____

Well, his
When his

bod - y's got the mo - tion and the rhy - thm's in ____ his feet. ____
bod - y's set in mo - tion, the la - dies cry a thou - sand tears. ____

Macho Duck

From Walt Disney Productions' *Mickey Mouse Disco*

Words and Music by Tom Worrall

Well, he's got style, __ and he's got flair, __ got two left feet __ but he does-n't care. __

__ Dressed in blue, __ fit to form; __ the la-dies love __ to touch his u - ni-form. __

__ Mess with him __ and you're out __ of luck. He's a ma-cho duck.

Chorus

Ma - cho, ma-cho duck,__ oh, he is a man-ly sen - sa -
Ma - cho, ma-cho duck,__ the slick - est__ bird in the na -

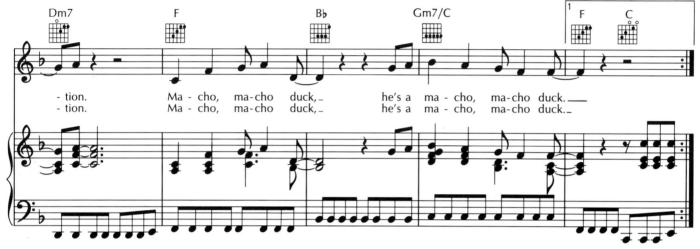

- tion. Ma - cho, ma-cho duck,__ he's a ma - cho, ma-cho duck.__
- tion. Ma - cho, ma-cho duck,__ he's a ma - cho, ma-cho duck.__

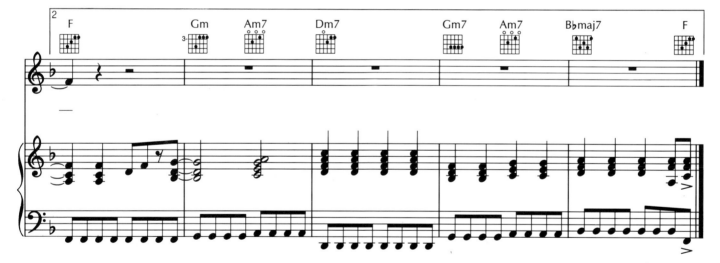

Additional verses

Can he move? Well, guess what?
He's got a wiggle and a waddle strut.
But feathers fly when he gets riled,
It's like a pillow fight that's gone wild.
Mess with him and you're out of luck.
He's a macho duck.

Builds his muscles, meets the test.
Gots lots of feathers on his chest.
He's laid back, he's in demand,
But he's really hard to understand.
Mess with him and you're out of luck.
He's a macho duck.

To Chorus

To Chorus

Best of Friends

From Walt Disney Productions'
The Fox and the Hound

Words by Stan Fidel
Music by Richard Johnston

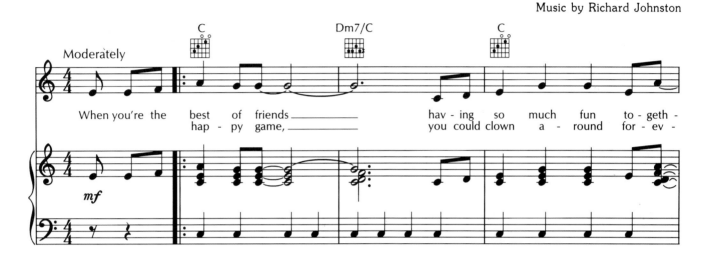

Lyrics:

When you're the best of friends _____ hav-ing so much fun to-geth-
hap-py game, _____ you could clown a-round for-ev-

-er, you're not e-ven a-ware _____ you're such a fun-ny pair. _____
-er. Nei-ther one of you sees _____ your nat-ur'l bound-a-ries. _____

You're the best _____ of friends. _____ Life's a Life's one hap-py game.

If on-ly the world would-n't get in the way,— if on-ly peo-ple would just let you play.

They'll say you're both be-ing fools, you're break-ing all— the rules.—

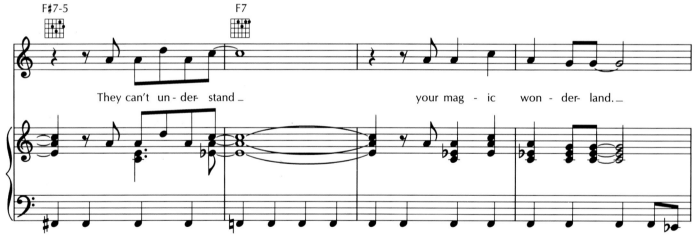

They can't un-der-stand — your mag-ic won-der-land.—

When you're the best of friends, ——— shar-ing

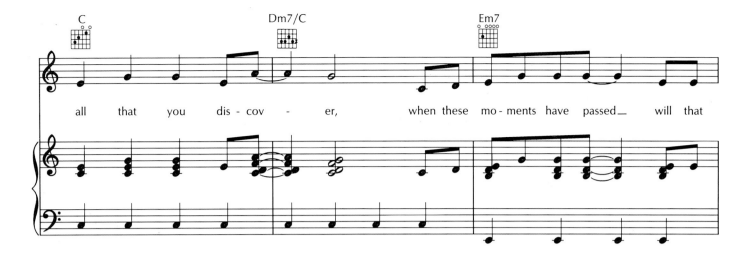

all that you dis-cov - er, when these mo - ments have passed__ will that

friend - ship last?__ Who can say__ if there's a way?__ How I hope,__

I hope it nev - er ends, _____ 'cause you're__ the

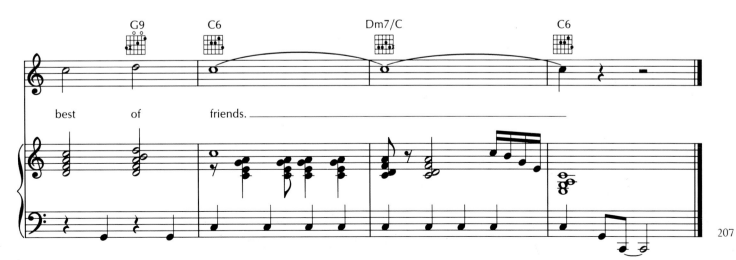

best of friends. _____

207

Happy Birthday

From Walt Disney Productions' *Splashdance*

Words by Michael Silversher
and Patricia Silversher
Music by Michael Silversher

208

209

Love Came for Me

From Walt Disney Productions' *Splash*

Words by Lee Holdridge
Music by Will Jennings

Song Index

258.3 257.11 261.3 262.11

XW-26 T-2

GOOF — HAPPY JABBER

13x

XW-10 T-3 S-5 (CONT)

HOW ABOUT A STRAWBERRY SHORTCAKE?

18x 6x

308.13 311.13

GOOFY JUMPS UP + DOWN — JABBERING

13x 6x

INT. DON OFFERS UP CAKE TO GOOF — GOOF REACTS HAPPILY

1x 22x

GOOF JUMPS UP + DOWN WITH JOY

20x Sc. 35-4x

167 5.14 168 (6-00) -04½ 169 1-12 170 FC 3-04

4 5 6 7

264.1 265.11 267.3 268.11

XW-26 T-2

(GOOF — HAPPY JABBER)

314.13 317.13

GOOF TAKES THE CAKE

8x 20x 9x 21x

REACHES UP FOR VINE SWINGS DOWN GOOF SWINGS THRU SC. 13x 19x

GRABS CAKE 14x DON NONCHALANTLY TAPS LIPS

20x Sc. 36-4x

171 4-12 172 (7-03) -04½ 173 1-12 174 3-04

8 9 10